iPhone

User Manual

For Dummies, Beginners & Seniors to Become Expert of iPhone XR and Upgrade iOS 12 to Latest iOS 14 to Benefit All Features in iPhone 12, Mini, Pro & Max 2020

Ephong Globright

Copyright © 2020

Facts Acclamation

This iPhone XR User Manual is primarily designed to provide complete solutions to several operational challenges on the use of many basic apps, technical setup, ensuring comfortability, and safe usage of the iPhone by the dummies, beginners, and seniors.

Table of Contents

3

5

INTRODUCTION

The iPhone XR Manual is majorly arranged and illustrated with many self-explanatory labeled pictures, screenshots, latest tips, and easy to do step by step technical problem solutions.

This user guide is awesomely suitable for a first-timer or a beginner in the use of iPhone that has a great desire of improving the level of enjoying mobile communication and innovative technology from Android phone to evergreen iPhone XR running with iOS 13 above by upgrading methods that were fully discussed in this informative and helpful iPhone XR User Manual Book.

More so, this inevitable Manual will completely guide dummies, beginners, and seniors that are new in the use of applicable techniques surrounding the successful operation of full-screen iPhone XR.

Definitely, senior users will find this iPhone XR user manual as an essential companion that will always provide a perfect quick solution to all his/her expectations.

In this book, the level of individual understanding of strange technological information was completely put into consideration by showing the location and the activities that will be done in the place.

Whether you are an aged or slow learner you will find this manual guide very beneficial because it is full of labeled pictures, screenshots and explained with simple English terms.

Therefore, all the complex (tough) technological terms had been completely translated into simplified words that every user or user-to-be could understand easily without looking for someone to assist him or her for more interpretation.

It is of my happiness to hear from all beneficiaries of this iPhone XR User Manual that they can solve all their problems on their iPhones completely without any difficulty.

The Full Component of iPhone XR

iPhone XR was the next advanced full-screen iPhone that was produced and released with iPhone XS, and iPhone XS Max by Apple Company on September 12, 2018, which was a year after the production of the first full-screen iPhone X that came with iPhone Operation System 11 (iOS 11), but the iPhone XR came with iPhone Operating System 12 (iOS 12) which is faster and loaded with many attractive features of different applications (apps) with great satisfaction.

Why You Need iOS?

iPhone Operation System (iOS) is the major designed software (untouchable internal programming) for iPhone that gives opportunities for all the general activities that users could perform on iPhone through the operational tools called "Applications (Apps)".

Why You Need Apps?

All the Apps on iPhone XR have different features that will enable you to do all the necessary things you wanted to perform on your iPhone. Further, each app has a separate representative logo that is called **Icon.** The icon will enable you to know the App you are looking for and the App that has a particular function to provide a solution to a certain problem.

For instance, Phone App can be identified with this Icon on the home screen of your iPhone that you can use to make or receive a call.

What Are the Available Apps' Icons?

The available Apps' Icons on the iPhone XR Home screen that has been upgraded from iOS 12 to iOS 13 are stated below:

Messages, 9 *Calendar,* *Photos,* *Camera,* *Weather,* *Clock,* *Maps,* *FaceTime,* *Notes,* *Reminder,* *Stocks,* *News,* *Home,* *iTune Store,* *Apple Store,*

Books, ♥*Health,* ▢*Wallet,* ◉ *Settings,* ◉*Podcast,*
Phone, ✉*Mail,* ✦ *Safari,* ♫ *Music,* ◉ *Find My,* ◉*Shortcuts,*
◉*Contacts,* ◉*Compass,* ▦*Measure,* ▦ *Calculator,* ▭
Files, ◉*Watch, and* ◉*Tips.*

You can still request more apps on your iPhone through Apple Store freely. More apps you can get from the Apple store are *iMovie, iTunes Remote, iTunes U, Number, GarageBand, Clips, Keynote, Pages, and Music Memos.*

All the above apps are very important for you to fully benefit the operational efficiency of your iPhone and make life very simple to explore and achievable. **The most important and inevitable Apps that you must know the beneficial features are: Settings, Call, Messages, Camera, Photo, FaceTime, Siri, Safari, Mail, and Music.**

Settings: This app will enable you to access the settings of all the available apps on your iPhone. Through the Settings app, you can perfectly activate all the essential apps (e.g. Face ID, Siri, Passcode, Wi-Fi Network, iCloud, etc.) that you are unable to or skipped during your iPhone setup.

Phone: This will enable you to reach out to your friends or loved ones that you are having their **contact** details on your iPhone. The phone app will enable you to receive or make a call.

Massage: This will enable you to send text messages to your loved ones in your contacts. You have two ways of sending a message to people.

1. SMS or MMS
2. iMessage

SMS or MMS: You can send a text message through SMS and MMS to anyone on your contact that is using an Android phone. The sending button is green.

iMessage: This is a live interactive message medium that will enable you to see when the person you are sending your text message to is typing his/her messages. It is only available for those who are using an iPhone. The sending icon is blue.

Camera: This will enable you to take new pictures or images and record videos of any event. In it, there is image-beatifying features that can be applied to edit and modify the image output.

Photos: In this app, you can fully access all your saved pictures regarding time, day, month, location, and event. This app will arrange and indicate the source of store images such as *Screenshot, WhatsApp, Facebook, Video, Movies, DCIM, Camera, Live Pictures...and others.* You can add labels to any specific event photographs.

FaceTime: As the name of the app implies **FaceTime** will enable you to make face-to-face calls, audio calls, live to chat text messages on your iPhone with the use of the latest Animoji or customized, Memoji and Emoji.

Siri: This app is a wonderful work executor and apps, problem solver. It serves as a messenger or personal assistant to help you determine several activities associated with other apps on your iPhone. It can help you set and save time in Alarm, a reminder for events, check daily weather/climatic conditions, recall the missed calls or messages and it can also help you compose messages and send them to whosoever you want to send them to.

If you call its attention, it will do anything you want it to do for you. Its voice could be set to female or male voice depending on your choice. It is one of the great successes ever apple has achieved in using technology to solve the iPhone user's bothering issues with ease.

How to talk to Siri

Safari: This app is used to browse for any information

online or to download more applications, games, dictionaries, music, videos, language translator, WhatsApp, Facebook... and many others.

Mail: The App will enable you to instantly access your received email messages and to reply to messages.

Music: This app will enable you to play any audio music in your music library.

Health: This is an amazing app that you can use to track everything about your health to ensure your daily general wellbeing. You can also use it to monitor your daily food consumption through the regulation of calories and monthly menstrual cycle in women; heart condition, fasting discipline, sleeping status, working ability... and many other activities essential to your comfortable life.

Find My: This App is very important to either quickly locate your misplaced iPhone or retrieve suspected lost iPhone without using a Wi-Fi network or Cellular connection even when the battery is done you can still recover your lost iPhone.

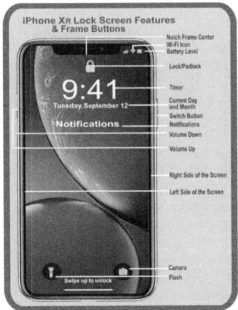

What are the Major iPhone Screens?

The major screens of your iPhone are called **Lock Screen** and **Home Screen.**

Lock Screen: This is an entry screen that contains a timer, date, notification, camera icon, cellular icon, Wi-Fi network icon, battery icon, flash icon, and security lock.

The most important features of the icons on the

Lock screen are:

Timer: It automatically set itself with the most accurate regional global time of your location. It instantly determines regional timing.

Notifications: It strictly works by your instruction to determine the information that will be shown on the Lock screen.

But, by default, it could display all information regarding calls, emails, messages, alerts, and alarm notifications. However, you may restrict the exposure of your messages or mail detail from the Lock screen in the notification settings to prevent anyone from seeing your privacy.

You have to unlock your iPhone before you can perform the following:

Flash: You can use the flash at the bottom left of the Lock screen to lighten the dark environment and facilitate the sharp and clear output of pictures taken in uniformly dark surroundings.

Camera: It can be constantly used to perform video image capturing and picture taking without you navigating through the Homescreen.

You could swipe from the right side of the iPhone to launch the Camera page or press the Switch button to access Camera and click on any of the down or up buttons for the volume at the left side of the iPhone to take a shot if you don't want to use Shutter on the Camera interface.

Apps Searching Tool: When you slide your iPhone from the left side you will see searching tools that will enable you to find many apps information about your iPhone. Ask more of Apple store, iCloud, or Siri to have full knowledge of them. There is much informative news that is displaced below that you can tap on to read details.

Place your finger at the bottom of the Notch frame center of your iPhone and slightly move down your finger you will see a searching field with suggested favorite Apps that you can navigate to get what you need on the iPhone.

But, if the app you are looking for is not among the suggested apps, you can further type in the app into the searching field for easy access.

Hint: Whenever you see **Search or Text Field** on your iPhone without seeing any Keyboard to type text into the field. All you need to do is to initially tap on the surface of the **Search or Text field**, immediately Keyboard will appear below for you to enter your search text keywords into the field. Examples of apps that contain text fields are Mail, Messages, Safari, or other Browsers, Camera, Call Contact, Calendar, FaceTime, Health... and many others.

Control Center: You can view Control Center from the Lock screen. Swipe down from the right side of the Notch at the center top of your iPhone.

The security padlock will be unlocked through your **Face Identity (ID)** if you have done the Face ID during the iPhone Setup. A blinking infra-red sensor will be showing from the **Notch** at the top center of your iPhone and once you look at the Lock screen, your

face will be scanned and the locked padlock will open for you to access the Home screen by swiping up from the bottom center of the screen.

Home Screen: This is the second screen that also contained a timer, cellular icon, Wi-Fi network icon, battery icon, and all the Apps I have mentioned above.

The Apps occupy two screen pages that you can see when you swipe the Home screen from right to left.

How You Can Know All the External Parts of the iPhone XR

The Complete Physical Appearance of Your iPhone XR

General Front & Back Views of iPhone XR

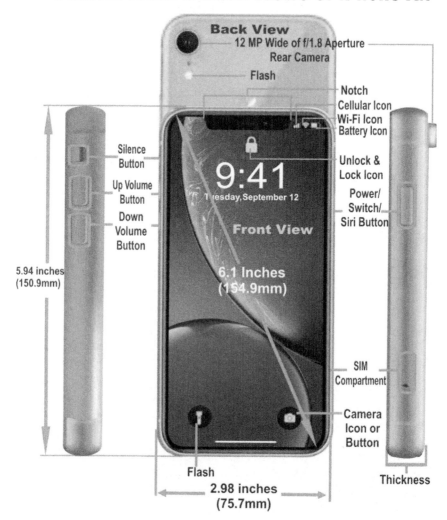

What is the Use of Notch?

A notch is a black compartment at the top center of the iPhone that contains many **Sensors** like *Infrared sensors, Flood Illuminator, Proximity Sensor and Ambient Light Sensor*; **Microphone, Speaker, 7MP Front-Facing Camera of depth field f/2.2 aperture, and Dot Projector**.

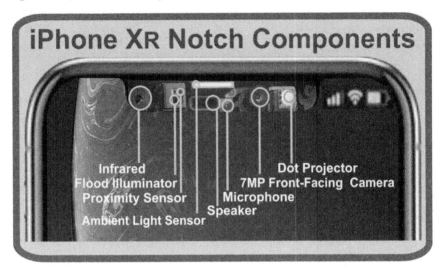

The Microphone will help to improve your voice when you are making a call or voice recording.

The Speaker will help you hear sound loud and clear through the out-speaker. You may listen to the audio, voice without using earpieces or earphones, or headphones.

The 7MP Front-Facing Camera could quickly enable you to take selfies. The camera at the front of your iPhone which is called the *Front-Facing Camera* comes with TrueDepth of 7MP of a small focus of depth field f/2.2 aperture with a resolution of 1080p HD for video recording and picture capture.

The Rear Camera is the camera at the back of your iPhone XR. iPhone XR comes with a single Wide Camera which is 12MP Wide with a small focus of depth field f/1.8 aperture.

Video Playback: The iPhone XR can be prettily used to play HDR10 content and Dolby Vision HDR.

Zoom Magnification: You can zoom out images 10 times the original image on your camera screen and zoom in the image up to two times the original image on iPhone XR.

Portrait Mode: The Portrait effect in the Camera capture is Depth Regulation and Advanced Bokeh that can further be beautified with Filter and 3 Portrait Lighting Effects which include Natural, Studio & Contour.

Audio Playback: The iPhone XR can be used for Stereo Playback.

Battery Durability: iPhone XR has a strength of 2942mAh – Lion of 3.8V with a strong and long-lasting battery capacity that can enable you to perform long activities. It is 1hour 30 minutes stronger than iPhone 7. On many occasions, the rate of battery discharge depends on many activities you are performing on your iPhone XR and the time you use to do them. If you are doing many functions or you use the iPhone for a longer time than usual it may reduce the battery durability.

➢ **Video Playback:** iPhone XR can closely last 16hours to make Video Playback.

➢ **Audio Playback:** At a stretch, your iPhone can endure 65hours in making Audio Playback; what a fantastic durable satisfaction.

Battery Maintenance Facts:

1. When you have fully charged your iPhone XR battery, remove it from the source of light before you start operating the iPhone.

2. Ensure you have used the battery to 40-30% charged before you connect it to the source of electricity to recharge your iPhone XR battery.
3. Always avoid your iPhone XR battery from being completely discharged or rundown to 5 or 0% before you recharge it.
4. Do not allow the iPhone XR to suddenly trip off because the battery has been discharged.
5. Set battery percentage limit and battery protective move on your iPhone to provide your iPhone a long time to use it.
6. If you want to carry out a setup or uploading or downloading or recording on your iPhone and it will take too much time that the current battery level cannot complete it, immediately, connect it to the source of electricity to boost the battery capacity and once it is fully charged, then disconnect the iPhone XR from the USB lightning cable and continue your activity.

How You Can Connect Lightning to USB Cable and Adapter to Charge iPhone XR

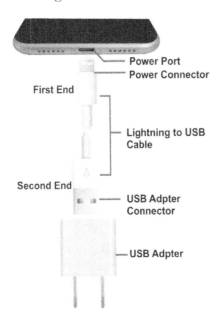

In the package of the iPhone XR, you will see a Lightning to USB Cable, an Adapter of 18 Watt, a Pair of Earpod with a connecting cable, and a SIM Card Tray Ejector.

First Step: Take the first end of the lightning to USB Cable and insert it into the iPhone Power Port under the bottom of the iPhone XR.

Second Step: Take the second end of the lightning to the USB Cable and insert the USB connector into the USB lightning adapter port at the head of the Adapter.

Third Step: Plug the USB Adapter pins inside an electric Plug socket and switch on the button of the plug.

Hint: Within a few seconds charging batteries with the percentage charged will show on the screen for you to know that the iPhone XR is effectively

53% Charged

charging. But, if you wait for about a minute without seeing the battery charging icon come up, adjust the adapter connected with the main plug of the source of electricity.

iPhone XR Body Dimension: The height of the is 5.94 inches (150.9mm); the breadth (width) is 2.98 inches (75.7mm): the weight is 6.84 ounces (194g); the high definition (HD) screen display diameter is 6.1 inches Liquid Regina HD, and thickness is 0.33 inch (8.3mm).

Different Memory Storage Capacity: iPhone XR come with different storage capacities of 64 GB and 128 GB (Gigabyte) that determine the price of the iPhone XR. The storage capacity is the space that is naturally available on your iPhone. The more the space capacity the more data or documents you can store on your iPhone storage. Therefore, if you go for iPhone XR with high storage capacity you will have an opportunity to have more data or documents on your iPhone XR, however, you can still support your iPhone storage with iCloud Storage to backup all your data and apps on your iPhone XR.

Random Access Memory: iPhone XR comes with 3 GB of Random Access Memory that majorly determines the speed of the iPhone in terms of performing, transferring, downloading, uploading, updating documents or data, and upgrading the iPhone Operating System on your iPhone XR.

Apple A12 Bionic Chip: It is a Chip that contains a 64-bit Acorn RISC Machine (ARM) System which is also called System on Chip (SoC). The Chip has two high efficient powers of 15% and 50% faster than the A11 Bionic Chip in iPhone X. The first-ever 7nm node of the chip system produced

18

by Apple Company to improve the rate of performing various activities on your iPhone without any delay.

Available & Compatible Wireless &Cellular: iPhone XR is compatible with EDGE or GSM, DC-HSPA+, LITE Advanced, HSPA+, or UMTS, few models of CDMA EV-DO Rev. A, Bluetooth 5.0, Express Cards, In-Built of GNSS or GPS, 802.11ac Wi-Fi with MIMO and NFC with reader mode.

IP68 Certification: iPhone XR has just a 30-minute resistant ability to endure 1 meter of water depth. It is not advisable to deliberately put your iPhone XR in water that you do not know the depth of the water. It is only satisfied with the 1-meter depth of water not more than that. More also, iPhone XR can survive in a dusty environment.

Documents You Can Access on Your iPhone XR

There are documents you can access on your iPhone XR without looking for a format converter. Any of the accepted documents can be used or shared on the website page, mail, social media platform or to compose a message on your iPhone as a reminder or planner… and many others.

The documents are:

1. Microsoft Excel of XISX and XIS
2. Microsoft PowerPoint of PPTX
3. Microsoft Word of DOCX and DOC
4. Text of TXT
5. Image of JPG, GIF, TIFF;
6. USDZ Universal of USDZ, ZIP, and ICS
7. Keynote of KEY
8. Preview and Adobe Acrobat Document Format of PDF
9. Contact information of VCF
10. Rich Text Format or RTF
11. Numbers of NUMBERS format.
12. Web Pages of HTML and HTM

How You Can Put Compatible SIM Card Into Your iPhone XR

You can use Nano-SIM and eSIM (Dual SIM) on your iPhone XR. There is a **SIM Tray Ejector** in the iPhone XR pack that you will use to eject the SIM Card tray from the right-hand side of the iPhone below the Power Button.

First Step: Let the front of your iPhone XR face up; with your hand, pick the Ejector and position it parallel/horizontal to the hole at the lower end of the SIM Card tray's cover.

Second Step: Insert the SIM Ejector into the small hole to touch the end surface inside and push the surface, immediately the SIM Card tray will partially come out.

Third Step: Use your hand to pull it out completely.

Fourth Step: Let the Circuit Steel surface (the front face) of your SIM Card face up and place the card on the tray according to the shape of the SIM. Do not position the SIM card against the shape designed on the SIM Tray. Do not turn the SIM face upside down.

Fifth Step: Insert the SIM Tray with SIM Card on it back to the SIM compartment as you removed it. Now you are through.

How You Can Solve Problem On iPhone In This Book

The pages that you will need to navigate through for you to get to where you are going on your iPhone were written in **bold font** with red color to call your attention.

After you have tapped on any app like the Settings app on the **Home screen,** you will see the next action to tap and that will be written in Bold Black font. If you are to continue, then you will see the first bold black word that will be written in bold red font on the second line and the next action will be written in bold black font.

Each bold red word represents each page title that you will see at the top of each page screen during settings.

For example, if you are going to Camera Settings.

On Homescreen: Tap on the **Setting Icon** (First Line of Action).

On Settings: Scroll down to select **Camera** (Second Line of Action).

On the first line of action, you will see Homescreen appears in red color which means the page name, while **Settings Icon** appears in black color which means "what you are looking for on the page (i.e. your mission)".

On the second line of action, the **Settings Icon** changes to Settings because at this stage you have launched the Settings page, therefore, the red color appearance of the Settings is representing the Settings page not "mission", while **Camera** is your next mission on the Settings page.

Meaning of Terms

Please get used to the meaning of the below simple terms I used in this book to help rapid learning and digestion of different technical steps.

Activator: It is used for the "switch button" to turn on/off apps features in Settings.　　 or

21

Activate: This means you should turn on the **Activator.**

Deactivate: This means you should turn off the **Activator.**

Regulator: It means **"Control"**. It has a round button on a parallel line that can be moved to either right or left to regulate the level of volume of a sound or light on your iPhone X<small>R</small> Settings.

Type: It means "Enter" words or numbers into a text or search field.

Text or Search Field: This is a place where you can type in words or numbers.

CHAPTER ONE

How You Can Automatically Setup your iPhone XR from Pack & Start Working

As a beginner, you need to provide all the needful requirements to ensure a successful iPhone XR setup. If you are previously using an Android phone and now you want to start using Apple iOS (iPhone Operating System), you have to first and foremost make your iPhone XR connect with Cellular Service Provider Network or effective Wi-Fi Network.

It may require you to activate your iPhone Bluetooth control in the control center. All these will help you to transfer your data and documents on an Android phone easily.

All the steps you will need to take to achieve your aims and objectives on your iPhone XR were sequentially arranged in this manual.

As a senior iPhone user, that has been using lower iPhone model before, and now you want to move to an advanced generation of iPhone model; you can start your iPhone XR set up manually if you know that you do not have much special data or documents to transfer from the old Android, however you may later transfer through data transferring method. It is optional.

But, if you virtually want all your data and documents on the old iPhone to be completely transferred into the new iPhone XR you will need to follow the automatic transferring setup of the iPhone XR that will be discussed after this manual setup with other important procedures that you must strictly follow to successfully set up your iPhone XR.

What To Do First

➤ When you remove the iPhone XR from the sealed pack, connect the lightning to the USB cord to the power port at the under bottom center of the iPhone.

➤ Connect the other USB end to 18 Watt USB port adapter at the head and plug it into the electric source to charge the iPhone.

➤ If you are having Computer, you can connect the USD connector of the cable to your fully charge Computer USB port.

➤ On the iPhone screen, the current battery charged will appear. Once it is fully charged disconnect your iPhone XR from the source of electricity.

➤ Insert your SIM card according to the method you have been told earlier.

➤ Protect the iPhone casing with a nice iPhone XR case and screen protector.

Do you have videos, audio music or messages, photos, or any other essential documents you want to transfer from your Personal Computer or Android Phone during Setup?

➤ Turn On the Wi-Fi network on your Android or PC containing the data or documents you wanted to transfer into your new iPhone XR.

➤ Rename the Wi-Fi ID on your Android or Computer Wi-Fi settings to ease the recognition of your iPhone XR. (Optional).

➤ Endure the Network is active and ensure that the Android or PC is fully charged.

If you want the document to be transferred automatically from your Android after you have finished the iPhone XR setup automatically, then you must initially do the settings below on your iPhone XR to prevent failure of document transfer.

Do These Settings on Your iPhone XR

✓ Enable Bluetooth
✓ Enable Cellular connection & Wi-Fi Network

- ✓ Ensure you enter the correct Apple ID
- ✓ Enable "*Find My iPhone*" Settings.
- ✓ Recharged your iPhone Battery
- ✓ Ensure there is enough storage space that will take all the documents you wanted to transfer on your new iPhone. But if you do not have enough you can buy more memory storage from iCloud.

How to Make Your Old iPhone Ready for Automatic Data and Apps Transfer

What May Affect the Transfer of the Data & Apps are:

- ✓ Off Bluetooth or Bad Rear Camera Sensor
- ✓ Poor Cellular connection or Wi-Fi Network
- ✓ Entering of Incorrect Apple ID
- ✓ Activation of "*Find My iPhone*" Settings.
- ✓ Low Charged Battery

Low Storage Space (it make slow down the speed)

What to do first

There is a need for some little steps of apps' activations through settings on your old iPhone before you continue to move all the data and documents into the new iPhone XR.

The first things to do on your old iPhone are:

- ➢ Go to Control Center on your iPhone, tap on the Cellular Service icon, Wi-Fi icon, and Bluetooth icon to turn them on.

If the Wi-Fi network is not responding or you have not turned on the Wi-Fi connection on your old iPhone before, then do the following steps to activate your old iPhone Personal Hotspot.

At the Homescreen: Tap on **Settings Icon**

In the Settings Page: Tap on **Personal Hotspot**

At the Hotspot Page:

1. Tap on the **Personal Hotspot** activation switch ⏤ to turn green.

2. On a displayed Wi-Fi and Bluetooth are Off Box tap on **Turn On Wi-Fi and Bluetooth.**

3. On the appearing Bluetooth Off Dialog Box, tap on **Wi-Fi and USB Only.**

4. Tap on Wi-Fi Password

Wi-Fi Password:

1. Tap on the **Password Text Field surface** and use the keyboard below on the page to enter your "**Wi-Fi Password**".

2. Tap on **Done** at the top right angle of the iPhone.

3. Tap on the **Home button** to return to the Homescreen. But, if your old iPhone is iPhone X above then swipe up from the bottom.

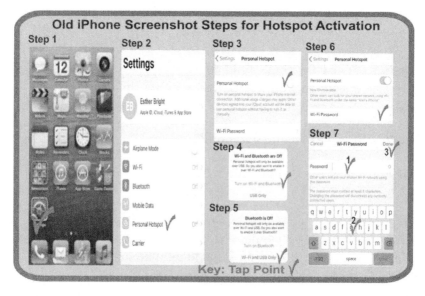

Now that the old iPhone Wi-Fi Network, Cellular Service, and Bluetooth were turned on and active, you can move to the next stage of moving data from the old iPhone to your new iPhone XR.

26

How To Position Old iPhone and New iPhone

You can either position the old iPhone on the right side of the new iPhone or the left side of the new iPhone, but what is very important is that they should not be too far from each other.

If you are a lefty/left-hand using person, you can position the new iPhone at the left side of the old iPhone.

But, if you are a righty/right-hand using person, position the new iPhone at the right side of the old iPhone because you will perform more installation tasks on the new iPhone than the old iPhone.

Make sure that the distance is 1 to 3cm between each of them or put your finger in between the new and the old iPhone to determine the distance.

You may put your SIM card later but make sure the battery is 100% charged before you start.

For example: In this cool guide, I transferred data and apps from iPhone 6 running iOS 11 to my newly purchased iPhone XR.

Hint: You must upgrade your old iPhone iOS to 11 to enable the transfer of the data and document.

How to Secure Your Old iPhone for New iPhone XR to Recognize

Save all your data with iCloud secured storage backup by navigating through:

At the Homescreen – Tap on the **Settings** icon

In the Settings – Tap on your **Name Profile** beside the Picture profile at the top.

27

At the Apple ID – Tap on **iCloud**

In the iCloud – Scroll downward and tap the **iCloud Backup** activation button  to put on the iCloud Backup.

Backup – Tap on **Back Up Now** to start the iCloud Backup.

At the Home Button – Click on the Home Button at the bottom center of the iPhone to go back to the Home screen immediately. Now you can start the setup process below.

Start The New iPhone Automatic Set Up Approach

1. Positioning
   ➢ Place both old and new iPhones beside each other on a table.
2. On Old iPhone
   ➢ Unlock the old iPhone and let it be on Homescreen.
3. On New iPhone
   ➢ Look at the right side of the new iPhone you will see a **Power button**, Press down till you will see a big word of **Hello** come up. The Hello will be changing from one language to another language on the screen
   ➢ Swipe up the screen from the bottom.
   ➢ Select your language.
   ➢ Select your region/country, within a second your new

28

iPhone will be seen on the screen of the old iPhone.

4. **On Your Old iPhone, You Will See** "Set Up New iPhone"

➢ Under the new iPhone's image Tap on the **Continue** bar.

➢ Within a second, a round white shape Camera space (i.e. Viewfinder) will come up for you to scan the moving coded circular eruption.

➢ Take the old iPhone above the new iPhone; let the rear Camera focus on the moving coded circular eruption, to be viewed in the center of the round **Viewfinder** on the old iPhone above.

➢ Be patient till you will see **"Finish on the New iPhone"** in the old iPhone before you will return it to its formal position.

While the old iPhone is transferring the information into the new iPhone, go to the new iPhone to continue the setup.

5. **On The New iPhone** "Enter Passcode of Other iPhone"

➢ Type the Passcode of your old iPhone without making a mistake. **"Setting Up Your iPhone"** will show on the screen. Wait till you will see the Face ID page.

29

6. On Face ID Page
   - ➢ Tap on the **Continue** bar.
   - ➢ Tap on the "**Get Started**" bar
   - ➢ Focus your eyes on the Front-Facing Camera Sensor and let your head be in the middle of the **Viewfinder** on the screen.
   - ➢ As you are turning your head gradually the surrounding lines of the **Viewfinder** will be changing to green, keep turning your head and let every side of your head be captured by the Camera sensor till the surrounding lines are completely changed to green.
   - ➢ If the first Face ID scanner is successful, Tap on the **Continue** bar and move your head in either the same or opposite ways, once the second Face ID scanner is complete another page will show and tell you that "**Face ID is Now Set-Up**"
   - ➢ Tap on the **Continue** bar
7. Alternatively, If you do not want to set up Face ID now, do the following:
   - ➢ Tap on the second option "**Set Up Later in Settings**".
8. Transfer Your Data
   - ➢ Tap on **Transfer from iPhone.** If you have updated all your apps and data, then you are good to go.
   - ➢ You may also choose **Transfer from iCloud** if you

are very sure that it is up to date. You may tap on **Other Options** to select any other device like Mac, PC, etc.

9. Terms and Condition

   Read through the terms and conditions on how to successfully use your iPhone and follow them strictly. Tap on the **Agree** option at the downright area of the screen.

10. Settings From Other iPhone

    ➢ Tap on the **Continue** option to proceed.

11. Keep Your iPhone Up to Date

    ➢ Choose the below option "**Install Update Manually**".

12. Apple Pay

    Enter your Apple Wallet detail if it is available with you by tapping on the **Continue** option.

    But, if you don't have one, choose "**Set Up Later in Wallet**" option below.

13. Apple Watch

    ➢ Tap on "**Set Up Later**" under the continue bar to proceed.

14. Apple Analytics

    Select the "**Don't Share**" option below Share with App Developers. The next interface will show you how the data is moving from your old iPhone to the new iPhone.

15. On Your Old iPhone

    When all the data are completely moved into your new iPhone XR, it will show on the interface of the old iPhone that "**Transfer Complete**".

    Tap on the **Continue** bar to enter the Homescreen of your old iPhone.

16. On New iPhone

    The New iPhone will show

Apple's image on the screen. After a while, it will change the screen appears to a white interface. Swipe Up the screen from the bottom center to launch into the data-loading Apple image interface.

You have to sufficiently endure enough to allow all the data and apps to completely move from the old iPhone into the new iPhone because the uncompleted Apps will appear black with a faded icon image on the Home screen of the new iPhone.

You will only see the icons that are completely loaded on your new iPhone XR screen as they have appeared on your old iPhone.

How You Can Manually Setup your iPhone XR after Purchase & Start Working

What To Do First

➢ When you remove the iPhone XR from the sealed pack, connect the lightning to the USB cord to the power port at the under bottom center of the iPhone.

➢ Connect the other USB end to 18 Watt USB port adapter at the head and plug it into the electric source to charge the iPhone.

➢ If you are having Computer, you can connect the USD connector of the cable to your fully charge Computer USB port.

➢ On the iPhone screen, the current battery charged will appear. Once it is fully charged disconnect your iPhone XR from the source of electricity.

➢ Insert your SIM card according to the method you have been told earlier.

➢ Protect the iPhone casing with a nice iPhone XR case and screen protector.

Do you have videos, audio music or messages, photos, or any other essential documents you want to transfer from your Personal Computer or Android Phone?

> ➤ Turn On the Wi-Fi network on your Android or PC containing the data or documents you wanted to transfer into your new iPhone XR.
> ➤ Rename the Wi-Fi ID on your Android or Computer Wi-Fi settings to ease the recognition on your iPhone XR. (Optional).
> ➤ Endure the Network is active and ensure that the Android or PC is fully charged.

Now you can take a further step of activating your newly purchased iPhone XR through manual setup.

1. Power Switch Button
   Look at the right side of the new iPhone you will see a button, Press down till you will see a big word of **Hello** come up. The Hello will be changing from one language to another language on the screen.

2. Hello
   Swipe up from the bottom center to tap on your **Language**.

3. Select Your Country or Region
   Scroll down to tap on your **Country.**

4. Quick Start
   On the bottom side of the screen tap on "**Set Up Manually**".

5. Choose a Wi-Fi Network
   Tap on the name of your "**Wi-Fi Source**".

6. Enter Password
   Enter the correct password of the "**Wi-Fi Network**" and tap on **Join** at the top right side of the screen.

7. Data & Privacy

Tap the **Continue** bar

8. Face ID
   a. Tap on the **Continue** bar.
   b. Tap on the "**Get Started**" bar.
   c. Focus your eyes on the Front-Facing Camera Sensor and let your head be in the middle of the **Viewfinder** on the screen.
   d. As you are turning your head gradually the surrounding lines of the **Viewfinder** will be changing to green, keep turning your head and let every side of your head be captured by the Camera sensor till the surrounding lines are completely changed to green.
   e. If the Face ID is successful, a **Continue** page will display. tap the **Continue** bar.

9. For later Face ID Settings hit the second option "**Set Up Later in Settings**".

10. Create a Passcode
    Use the Keypad to type complex **Passcode.** But, if you are not prepared, then tap on **Passcode Options** and tap on "**Don't Use Passcode**".

11. Passcode Box
    Tap on "**Don't Use Passcode**".

12. Apps & Data
    If you are having data on Android Phone you can tap on the option **Move Data from Android. Other options** are:
    a. Restore from iCloud Backup
    b. Restore from Mac or PC
    c. Don't Transfer Apps & Data

13. Apple ID
    a. Tap on the Text Field, use the Keyboard to type your Email address
    b. Tap on **Next** at the top right corner side.

c. Type in a correct **Apple Password** inside the text field.

d. Tap on **Next** at the top right corner side.

14. Apple ID Security

Tap the **Continue** bar to register your **Phone Number.**
But, if you do not want that to be done during setup, then you can tap on **Other Options.**
Tap on "**Don't Upgrade**" on the **Request Dialog Box.**

15. Terms and Condition

Read through the terms and conditions on how you can successfully use your iPhone and follow them strictly. Tap on the **Agree** option at the bottom right side of the screen.

16. Express Settings

Tap **Continue** bar below

17. Keep Your iPhone Up to Date

Choose the below option of "**Install Update Manually**".

18. Apple Pay

Enter your Apple Wallet detail if it is available with you by tapping on the **Continue** bar.
But, if you don't have one, choose the "**Set Up Later in Wallet**" option below.

19. Siri

Tap on the **Continue** bar to register Siri (optional)
But, tap on "**Set Up Later in Settings**" to perform the full settings of Siri through the Settings process.

20. Screen Timer

Tap **Continue** bar (optional), it could be done later, therefore, for now, choose "**Set Up Later in Settings**".

21. Apple Analytics

Select the "**Don't Share**" option below Share with App Developers.

22. True Tone Display
Tap on the **Continue** bar.

23. Appearance
   a. Select the **Light** option to make the iPhone screen appear brighter.
   b. Tap **Continue** bar

24. Display Zoom
Tap on the **Standard** small circle to select it.
Tap on the **Continue** bar

25. Go Home
Tap on the **Continue** bar

26. Switch Between Recent Apps
Tap on the **Continue** bar

27. Quickly Access Controls
Tap on the **Continue** bar

28. Welcome to iPhone
Swipe up from the bottom middle of the screen to access the **Homepage.** If you create a Passcode during setup, the iPhone will ask you to enter your registered Passcode before you can launch into the Homescreen.

Manual Setup for A New iPhone XR to Start Working

37

Manual Setup for A New iPhone XR to Start Working

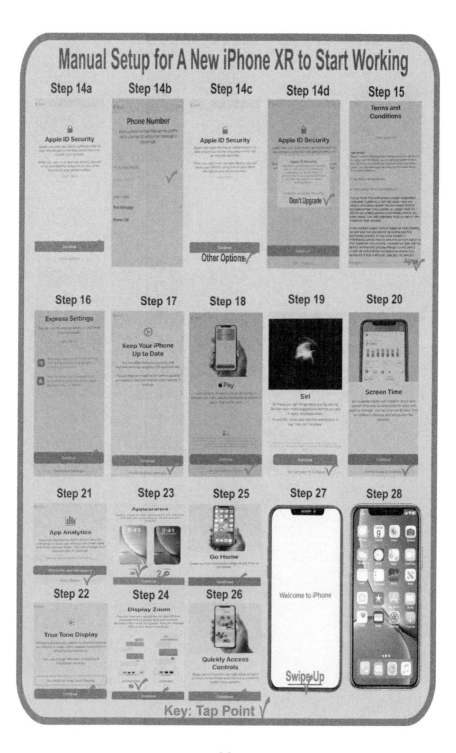

Step 14a — Apple ID Security

Step 14b — Phone Number

Step 14c — Apple ID Security

Step 14d — Apple ID Security — Don't Upgrade

Step 15 — Terms and Conditions — Agree

Step 16 — Express Settings

Step 17 — Keep Your iPhone Up to Date

Step 18 — Pay

Step 19 — Siri

Step 20 — Screen Time

Step 21 — App Analytics

Step 22 — True Tone Display

Step 23 — Appearance

Step 24 — Display Zoom

Step 25 — Go Home

Step 26 — Quickly Access Controls

Step 27 — Welcome to iPhone — Swipe Up

Step 28

Key: Tap Point

For Android User to Transfer Data and Vital Documents into iPhone XR

As a beginner in the use of the iPhone, you need to upgrade all your previous data and apps on your Android phone.

✓ You should also make sure that your Android Phone Battery and iPhone Battery are 100% charged.
✓ Use a strong Wi-Fi Network and turn On your Bluetooth. Alternatively, you can initially do the manual setup of the new iPhone for you to use the new iPhone Hotspot Wi-Fi Connection on your Android to fast track the data or document transfer.

Take these steps on your old Android Phone

On Homescreen

❯ Tap on the **Google Play Icon.**

On Google Play

❯ Tap on the **Google Play** at the top of the page
❯ Use Keyboard to enter **Move to iOS** and tap on the suggested Move to iOS keyword dropdown.

Move to 1OS Interface

❯ Tap on the **Open** bar
❯ Do not tap on **Continue** until you are on the page of Apps & Data on the new iPhone; where you will first tap on "**Move Data from Android**".

⟶ iOS Move from Android **on New iPhone**

❯ Tap on **Continue** below
❯ Enter the "**Code**" that shows on the screen of your iPhone into your Android phone.

Pick Up Your Android Phone at This Stable Page of Move to iOS

39

➢ Tap on the **Continue** above the phone image.

➢ Tap on **Agree**

➢ Tap on **Next** at the top right corner of the screen.

➢ Use the Keypad to enter the **Code** on the iPhone into your Android Phone.

Note: If you have taken too much time before you enter the code into your Android Phone, the transfer may be impossible.

If you experienced an unsuccessful transfer of data, immediately, tap on **Back** at the top left corner of the iPhone screen and re-tap on **Continue** to get another code. Enter the code fast into your Android Phone.

As soon as the transfer is complete on your new iPhone then tap on "**Continue Setting Up iPhone**".

Continue your iPhone setup steps from Step 13 above to complete the iPhone setup.

How You Can Upgrade iOS 12 on Your iPhone XR to Latest iOS 15 Version

It is of great advantage to upgrade the current iOS 12 on your iPhone XR to the current version of iOS 14 or 15 for you to benefit more of the latest features loaded in other advanced iPhones like iPhone 11, 11 Pro, 11 Pro Max, Second Generation iPhone SE running iOS 13; or iPhone 12 Mini, 12, 12 Pro & 12 Pro Max using iOS 14 or 13 Pro & 13 Pro Max using iOS 15 with high-speed efficiency.

Things You Must Put In Place Before You Get Started

➢ Get an effective Wi-Fi network.
➢ Confirm the available storage space on your iPhone XR. If you do not have up to 90 GB you can purchase from the iCloud store for more storage.
➢ Use iCloud or Mac or PC to back up all the data and documents on your iPhone.
➢ Charge your iPhone XR, and Mac or PC. You may connect your iPhone or upgrading device to a power source overnight.
➢ Make your Password available.
➢ Good lightning to USB cord.

How to perform Backup and iOS Upgrade on Computer

The Operational System for Apple Macintosh Computer (Mac)

➢ macOS Catalina 10.15 or
➢ macOS Mojave 10.14 or lower version.

Note: If you do not have Mac, you may use a PC instead.

If your Mac is running with a low version of macOS Mojave you can quickly update your Mac by taking the following step on your Mac.

On App Menu:

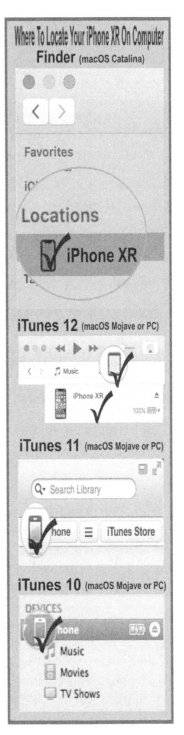

41

- Select **System Preferences** (operating system).
- Click on **Software Update** to look for an Updates
- Click on the **Update Now** option to install the latest version benefits. If you select **More Info** you will see full information on the individual update and choose the one you preferred later.
- Leave it for a while to completely install till you will see a message that "**your software is up to date**".

Now you can confidently move on to the update process of your iPhone XR on your newly updated Mac.

Step of iPhone XR Update on macOS Catalina 10.15

- Put On your Mac.
- Put On the Wi-Fi network connection on your Mac or PC

- Launch **Finder**

But if you are using a Mac running with macOS Mojave 10.14 or less, you will open **iTunes**

Step by Step of iPhone XR Update on macOS Catalina 10.15

- Use the lightning to USB Cable to connect your iPhone XR with a Mac USB port.
- Look at the left side of the Finder page you will see the image of your iPhone and the iPhone name under **Location.**
  - (If you have signed up your name with Apple ID, your first name will appear at the front of the iPhone image). Tap on the name of your iPhone.
  - Where you can locate your iPhone different from the iTunes version to another iTunes version in macOS Mojave and PC.
  - However, the location of your iPhone XR on iTunes 10 – 12 will be shown on the screenshot below.
- Once you click on your iPhone XR the Update provisional page for your iPhone will display on the right-hand side.

- ➤ Initially click on "**Back up all the data on your iPhone to this Mac**".
- ➤ Click on the "**Check for Update**".
- ➤ Click on the **Download** and **Update.**
- ➤ When you are asked to provide your **Passcode,** immediately type in your **Passcode.**
  The update will start, endure until the update is complete.
  Do not interrupt the update processing, because it is very important.

How to perform iOS Update on your New iPhone XR

On Homescreen:

- ➤ Place your finger at the top right of the iPhone screen and swipe down to launch **Control Center.**
- ➤ Hit on Cellular Service 🔘 and Wi-Fi network. 📶
- ➤ Swipe up from the bottom or tap the down plain of the screen to return to Homescreen.
- ➤ Tap on the **Settings Icon.** ⚙

On Settings: Scroll down to tap on **General**

On General: Tap on **Software Update.**

On Software Update: Select **Download** and **Install**

If your passcode is required then continue by:

Passcode: Type the correct **Passcode.**

Terms and Conditions: Select **Agree** at the lower right side to continue but if you mistakenly select **Disagree** it will discontinue the upgrade.

Immediately, the Upgrade will start, and you can let the iPhone upgrade overnight to finish the general processing because it always requires much time.

CHAPTER TWO

How You Can Use Default & Customized Controls On iPhone XR

Control Center is a unique swipe-down page that contains all the essential apps icon controls that you can quickly access on either iPhone Lock-Screen or Homescreen.

There are lots of apps with their operational icons on your iPhone Settings that can be customized to be in the Control Center for you to quickly access them.

Primarily, by default the following apps and operational icons are in your Control Center:

- ✓ Airplane Mode
- ✓ Cellular Service
- ✓ Wi-Fi Network
- ✓ Bluetooth
- ✓ Music Panel
- ✓ Screen Lock Rotation Icon
- ✓ Do Not Disturb
- ✓ Screen Mirroring Icon
- ✓ Screen Light Control (Contains True Tone & Night Shift)
- ✓ Volume Control

You can customize:

- ✓ Flash
- ✓ Timer
- ✓ Calculator
- ✓ Camera … and many others.

Airplane Mode Icon: It is used to keep your iPhone out of cellular service or network activity when you are on the Airplane board. It is activated when you tap on the icon surface.

Cellular Service Icon: It is used to activate the cellular service network provided by your SIM cellular provider. Tap on the surface of the icon to see the name of the network provider and active bar at the top left of your iPhone.

Wi-Fi Network Icon: This is a network data-using service that could be activated through **Personal Hotspot** in the Settings or received from an external device like iPhone/Android, Mac, iPad, or PC hotspot via Wi-Fi connectivity.

Bluetooth Icon: This is used to receive or transfer any app data or document from, or to other Bluetooth supporting devices. Tap the surface of the icon to activate the function. You can use it to send sound from your iPhone to another **Bluetooth** supporting sound device to play the sound aloud. You can send one document at a time.

Music Panel: You can use this to play and regulate the sound volume of music from your *YouTube* or iPhone music sound. Tap on the surface of the *Play Panel* to control the sound.

Screen Lock Rotation: This will prevent your iPhone screen display to instantly move from portrait to landscape at any quick repositioning of the iPhone to landscape. Tap the icon to permanent the portrait screen display but if you want to use your iPhone to watch the **video** you can re-tap the icon to deactivate the effect.

Do Not Disturb: You can use it to stop your iPhone from ringing, vibrating, and notifying you when you are in an important gathering, meeting, on the Airplane board, or driving a car.

Screen Mirroring Icon: This will enable you to see what is on the screen of your iPhone on your Mac, PC, Projector, or TV through the use of a specific cable connector.

Tap the surface of the icon to set the device connection and activate the application.

Screen Light Control: It is used to control the brightness and dimness of the screen light. If you want the screen light to be brighter, put your finger on the bright region of the control and move your finger up. But, if you want the screen face to look dim or dark move your finger from up to down.

When you press down the Light control, **Night Shift** the **True Tone** will appear below the screen.

You can further change the mode to **Night Shift** mode that will change the screen appearance to yellowish-cream like the evening period to protect sight (eyes).

Although by default (i.e. from the factory) it is set to **True Tone**, the icon activation appears blue.

Volume Control: It is used to control ring tone, alarm, video, or audio sound volume on your iPhone. Place your finger on the surface of the volume icon and high the volume by moving up your finger or lower the volume by moving down your finger.

Flash Icon: It is used to "On" **Touch/Flashlight** at the back of your iPhone. If you tap the **Flash icon** once immediately the Flashlight will display for you to see clearly or to make the back environment of your iPhone look like daylight and aids quick search.

Timer Icon: It is used to set various **Timer** formats and display the Timer on the **Homescreen.** Once you tap on the **Timer** icon you will access every detail of the **Timer Setting.**

Calculator Icon: It is used for adding, dividing, subtracting, and multiplying numbers in mathematical calculations like mathematician, accountant, statistician, or everyone, and it can be extensively changed to a scientific calculator for a scientist to calculate advanced calculations. Hit the **Calculator** icon for it to appear.

Camera Icon: It is quickly used to access a **Camera** page for you to take pictures and make videos. Tap on the Camera icon to get into the page instantly.

How You Can Add More Apps' Controls in Control Center

Customize Apps into Control Center

At the Homescreen: Tap on **Settings Icon.**

In the Settings Page: Scroll down and tap on **Control Center.**

In the Control Center

> ➤ Tap on the "**Customize Control**".
> ➤ You will see "**Access Within Apps**", put the activation button On ⬭ by tapping on the activator; if it is not previously activated.
> ➤ Tap on "**Customize Control**".

On Customize Control

> ➤ You will first see those controls that are in the Control Center listed above with a red circle having minus (remove) at the center that can be used to remove any of the controls from the Control Center if you deliberately want to remove any of the control. ⊖
> ➤ More listed Controls below are the available controls that you can add to those apps controls in the control center when you tap on the green circle having a cross sign (add) ⊕ at the center.

These are some of the controls you can add with those I have previously mentioned above:

47

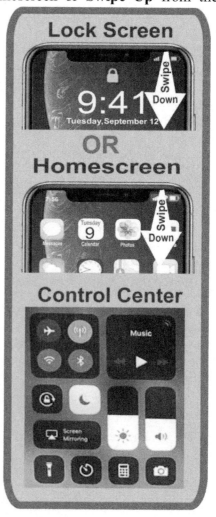

Accessibility Shortcut, <img> Apple TV Remote <img> Alarm, <img> Magnifier, <img> Text Size, <img> Note, <img> Guide Access, <img> Do Not Disturb While Driving, <img> Low Power Mode, <img> Voice Mail, <img> Stopwatch… and many others.

> Keep tapping on the **Back** icon at the top-left corner of the iPhone to return to Homescreen or **Swipe Up** from the bottom to return to Homescreen.

How You Can Create & Check Your Customized Controls from Control Center

View Controls on Lock Screen or Homescreen

> Position your finger at the top right side of your iPhone and swipe down

You will see the additional controls below those controls I have mentioned above.

If you do not see it, go back to *Customize Settings* to confirm if the control is still among the list of **Add More.** If you see it among the list, then tap on the **Add Circle** at the front of the control icon to add it.

If it is not among **Add More**

but among the list of those that are already in the control center then, revisit the control center by swiping down the screen of the iPhone from the top right side. Search carefully you will see it there.

How You Can Activate iPhone Screen Brightness from The Source

On Homescreen: Tap on the **Settings Icon**.

On Settings: Scroll down of the page to tap on **Display &**

Brightness  to access the settings.

Settings: Tap on the **Brightness** activation slide to become green.

> Slide the Brightness adjuster from left to right to increase the screen light or you slide the adjuster from right to left to reduce the screen light.

How Video and Music Can Be Taken from Other iPhones to Your iPhone XR

Settings on your iPhone and the other iPhone

On Homescreen

> Go to **Control Center,** turn On **Bluetooth** and tap the screen, or swipe up from the bottom center to go back to the Homepage.
> Tap on the **Settings App.**

On Settings: Tap on **General**

On General: Tap on **AirDrop**

On **AirDrop:** Select **Everyone** and swipe up for Home or continuously tap on the **Back icon** at the top left of the screen till you get to the Home page.

For iPhone Sending Video and Music (i.e. the iPhone Sending Video and Music)

On **Homescreen:**

> ➢ **Videos**
>> ✓ Tap on **Photos Icon** to pick the Video you want.
>> Or
> ➢ **Music**
>> ✓ Tap on **Music Icon** and select your preferred music.
> ➢ Tap on **Share Icon**
> ➢ Select **AirDrop** by tapping on it.

On Your iPhone

> ➢ Tap on **Accept** in the dialog option box of **AirDrop.**

On iPhone Sending Video and Music

> ➢ Tap on your iPhone Name that you are sending items to.

Instantly the new iPhone would receive the selected item.

How You Can Use iTunes App on Your iPhone XR

iTunes application is an important tool used in adding more pieces of stuff to your iPhone through your PC by sending and getting more pictures, music, video, etc. on your iPhone.

You can also use the iTunes Store to download many videos or music and play them offline on your iPhone with the use of a Wi-Fi connection. However, the service is not free, that is, you will pay for every requested music or audio at the iTunes store.

Sync your iPhone with iTunes to Get Additional Benefits

These are the following items you can add (sync) to iPhone from your iTunes library:

- ➤ Playlist,
- ➤ Movies,
- ➤ Songs,
- ➤ Podcasts,
- ➤ Album,
- ➤ Photo & Video,
- ➤ Audiobooks,
- ➤ Contact & Calendars.

You should sync your iPhone with iTunes if you want to include the below items on your iPhone:

- ➤ **iTunes Playlists** but you will initially subscribe with **iTunes Match or Apple Music.**
- ➤ **Personal Video**
- ➤ **Calendars, Photos,** and **Contacts** provided you are not using **iCloud.**

You can also use iTunes to delete the formally added items from your iPhone.

All those lively benefits can be downloaded from the iTunes Store without you passing through the PC connection.

For you to get the iTunes Store App on your iPhone freely by using Password take the following step.

On Homescreen

- ➤ Tap on **Settings Icon**

On Settings: Tap on your Name or Sign In and select the **iTunes & App Store.**

On iTunes & App Store: Tap on **Password Settings**

51

On **Password Settings**

> ➤ Switch on Face ID for buying all you need.
> ➤ Below PURCHASE AND IN-APP PURCHASE Tap on what you need.
> ➤ Below FREE DOWNLOAD you will see **Require Password**, Tap the activator to become Green.
> ➤ As soon as, you are requested to provide your **Password,** then enter it.
> ➤ Tap on **OK.**

How to Send Audio Sound to AirPlay Speaker from Your iPhone XR

On Homescreen: Go to **Control Center**

On Control Center: Tap on the **Screen Mirroring** icon

On Screen Mirroring: Press and hold the **Audio Card** for a few seconds and the **AirPlay** icon should be tapped on**.**

On AirPlay Speaker: Tap on the **AirPlay Speaker** to be connected.

Why You Need App Store on Your iPhone XR

You need app store your iPhone XR to enable you to download several apps and interactive social applications like Instagram, WhatsApp, Facebook, iMovie, Numbers, Keynote, Pages, GarageBand… and many others through the Apple store. To do this, tap on;

Homescreen: Tap on the **App Store** icon

On App Store: Tap on **Continue** bar.

Browsing Page: On a request optional box showing on your screen, tap on **Don't Allow** for Apple store not to access your location.

App Search: Look down at the lower left side of the screen to tap on **Search Icon.**

> ➤ Tap the search field to type in the app you desire.
> ➤ As soon as you see the App below, click on **"Get"** at the opposite for instant **Download**.
> ➤ Make Home **Swipe Up** to see the new App Icon.

How You Can Easily Solve iPhone Malfunctioning or Freezing Problem

Anytime you noticed that your iPhone has suddenly stopped working by not responding to touch and opening of the app(s). Do the following to restart your iPhone;

Stop carrying out any activities on the page you are.

At the Left Side of the iPhone;

> ➤ Click **Up-Volume** button
> ➤ Click the **Down-Volume** button.

At the Right Side of the iPhone

> ➤ Use 11 seconds to press the **Power Switch** button.
> ➤ The iPhone Switch Off and reboot itself to the Lock Screen.

At the Lock Screen

> ➤ Home Swipe Up.
> ➤ Provide your **Passcode**
> ➤ Home Swipe Up.

How You Can Fully Perform Notification Settings on Your iPhone XR

At the Homescreen: Tap on the **Settings** icon.

On Settings: Scroll down and tap on **Notification**

On Notification: Tap on the **App Store**

App Store: Give instructions to your iPhone by activating the following options **Allow Notification, Badge App, Show on Lock Screen, Show in History, and Show as Banner.**

> ➢ Tap on any of these options below:
>> ✓ **Temporary Banner Show**
>> ✓ **Persistent Banner Show**
> ➢ Make Home **Swipe Up.**

For Your iPhone Notification Preview

It is optional for you to choose where you want the notification preview to be shown when the iPhone is locked or unlocked. After the above steps, tap on the **Back** icon at the top left of the screen to return to the **Notification Page.**

On Notification: Select **Show Preview**

Show Preview: You may select **Always When Unlocked or Never.** But for privacy, you may tap on **When Unlocked.** This means it is only you that can see the notification(s).

How to Protect Cellular Data on Your iPhone XR

This will enable you to reduce and control the rate at which some apps consume data on your iPhone.

On Homescreen: Tap on the **Settings.**

On Settings: Select **Cellular.**

Cellular: Opposite **Cellular Data** tap on **Roaming Off.**

54

Turn On the activation switch of **Low Data Mode** to green.

How You Can Quickly Use Emergency Call to Prevent Predictable Danger on Your iPhone XR

This will make you get used to the instant ways of activating emergency provision and the quick approach of making an Emergency call when you notice danger or suspicious activities that may cause loss of treasure or life if you do not get urgent attention.

On Switch Button: Click the **Switch Button** 5 times.

On Homescreen: Tap on the **Settings Icon.**

On Settings: Move down to tap on **Emergency SOS**

On Emergency SOS: Tap on **Also Works with 5 Clicks.**

Anytime you notice a sudden attack or unforeseen danger, all you need to do is to quickly click the Switch Button 5 times and instantly you will be connected to **Emergency SOS.**

Other Method

Press down **Switch Button** and **Up Volume** together for the **Emergency SOS** screen to show up.

At the center of the screen, you will see **SOS Switch.** Slide the **SOS** Switch from left to right side to be connected to Emergency Call.

Hint: You can also switch off your iPhone on the same page by moving **Power Switch** from left to right.

CHAPTER THREE

How You Can Do Important Basic Futures On Your iPhone

How To Prevent Ringtone, Vibration, or Notification Alert

There are two major ways on your iPhone that you can use to prevent calls from ringing out or to avoid vibration or notification alerts or alarm sounds.

External Buttons

Silent Mode Button: This is the first small button on the left side of the iPhone that can be moved in the front and back direction.

Push the Button Back

When you move the small button from the front to the backside of the iPhone you will see red on the ground of the open and at the top of the screen, you will see a notification showing "**Silent Mode On**". This means that you have muted the iPhone, therefore, there will be no sound from a call, alarm, and notifications but it will vibrate if you have previously activated vibration during settings.

But, when you move the button from the back to the front of the iPhone the ring sound, alarm and notification alert sound will be restored.

Do Not Disturb

Lock Screen or Homescreen: Swipe down the screen from the top right side of your iPhone.

Do Not Disturb Icon: Tap on the **Do Not Disturb** control icon to stop ringtone and vibration from any call, message notification, alarm, and alert sound.

How To Initially Enable Do Not Disturb In The Settings

You will perform this in Settings to make the feature effective on your iPhone.

On Homescreen: Tap on the **Settings** icon

On Settings: Search down for **Do Not Disturb** and select it.

On Do Not Disturb: Tap on the activator button to change to green color.

Schedule Time You Don't Want To Be Disturbed By Anyone

If you schedule the time that you do not want people to disturb you with calls or messages then the above option (Do Not Disturb) will be deactivated automatically because you cannot use both features at the same time. You have to choose one.

Schedule: Tap on the Schedule, to set the time you don't want people to disturb you.

Specify Those Favorites That Your iPhone Can Allow

You have to choose some specific favorites that must be removed from **Do Not Disturb** instruction. The **Favorite Contacts** may be your Spouse, Children, Mother, Father, and Close Relative that may need your attention unexpectedly for any unforeseen Emergency.

Allow Calls From: Tap on the **Allow Call From** to select your favorites by tapping on the **Favorites** option.

Repeated Calls: Tap on the **Repeated Calls Activation Switch** to allow regular calls of your chosen favorites when you are busy till you pick the call.

Activate: Tap on **Activate** to select **Manually** from the below three available options:

1. Automatically
2. When Connected to Car Bluetooth
3. **Manually**

Manually you will always be able to activate **Do Not Disturb** through Control Center.

Auto-Reply To: Select **Auto-Reply** to choose the **Favorites** and **Auto-Reply Message** that will explain why you cannot pick up your iPhone presently.

Wake & Sleep Actions

The action will let your iPhone sleep and wake. If you are working on your iPhone and you quickly want to arrive at the **Lock Screen** without you making regular backing of pages to the Homepage.

What you will do is to click the **Power/Switch Button** on the right side of the iPhone. With just a click, the screen will fall asleep and when you make a click again on the same **Power Button** the iPhone will be awake at the **Lock Screen.**

Meanwhile, any of the security authentications like Face ID or Passcode may be required. If your Face ID failed your Passcode will be automatically displayed for you to enter.

Auto-Sleep

Your iPhone may sleep automatically if the idle time (the time you are doing anything) has passed the time frame you set in the Settings of the iPhone screen activities. Wake the screen by clicking the **Switch Button** to wake it on the same page you have stopped working.

How You Can Rearrange App's Icons on the Homescreen

You can move any app on the Home screen anywhere you prefer it to be. You may choose to arrange the apps in alphabetical order or base on the regular use of the apps.

On Homescreen: For a short time press the screen for a dialog box to appear.

Optional Box: Tap on the **Rearrange Apps** option. Immediately the entire apps will be stirring and unstable with the *Cancel sign* attached to the left top corner of each app.

Apps: Position your hand on each App you want to move and drag the app to the favorite place. As soon as, you are through with rearranging the Apps, **Swipe Up** the screen from the bottom.

How You Can Keep Two or More Apps' Icons In A File On Homescreen

Homescreen: For a short time press the screen for a dialog box to come up.

On the Dialog Box: Tap on the **Rearrange Apps** option. Immediately the entire apps will be

stirring and unstable with the *Cancel sign* attached to the left top angle of each app.

Apps: Position your hand on an App and drag it on another app to have the same file. Before you release the dragged App on the below App make sure that a transparent white square appears around the below app. You will see the File Name text field above, tap on the text field to name the file.

If you want more than 2 Apps in a file, then continue dragging Apps on the file you have created and tap on the external part of the file to restore and fix it.

As soon as you are through, **Swipe Up** the screen from the bottom, the whole apps will come back to normal.

How to Return the Apps to the Previous Position

Created File

> - **Two Apps in a File,** hold-down the file for a dialog box to show up for you to tap on **Rearrange Apps.** Immediately, the two Apps will be released from the file and shown as individual app on the Homescreen.
> - **More than Two Apps in a File,** hold-down the file to show a dialog box for you to tap on **Rearrange Apps** and all the Apps will be liberated.
> - **If you want to be taken the Apps out of the file one after the other:**
>   - ✓ Tap the file compartment and the whole Apps will be seen boldly.
>   - ✓ Place your finger on any of the App and drag it out. The file will contract back while the liberated App will be on its normal side.
> - **Swipe up** from the bottom to stabilize the apps.

How You Can Delete Apps at the Homescreen

On Homescreen

> ➢ Hold down the app until you will see an optional dialog box.
> ➢ Tap on the **Delete** option. Immediately the app will be removed. *OR*
> ➢ Hold down the app till the whole apps are stirring and unstable with a Cancel indication at the left angle of the apps.
> ➢ Tap on the **Cancel sign**. Immediately the app will be removed from the page and the whole apps will automatically rearrange itself.
> ➢ **Swipe Up** to stabilize the apps.

How You Can Choose More Attractive Wallpaper for Both Lock Screen & Home Screen

You can choose beautifully attractive Wallpaper from various Apple-designed wallpapers or your admirable photo. The Wallpaper is sectioned into four categories:

1. Dynamic Wallpaper
2. Still Wallpaper
3. Live Wallpaper
4. Photo Wallpaper

Dynamic Wallpaper: The wallpaper contains several circular bubbles in different sizes that slightly increase in size on the screen.

Still Wallpaper: The wallpapers comprise different designed stable images and natural pictures without movement.

Live Wallpaper: The wallpaper shows movement when you touch the screen. Any image that is chosen in this category for your either Lock screen or Homescreen moves when you press down the screen. You can preview the animation before you set it for either the Lock screen or Home screen.

On **Homescreen**: Tap on the **Settings** icon.

On **Settings**: Scroll down of the page and select **Wallpaper**

Wallpaper: Above the Lock Screen and Homescreen Image tap on **Choose A New Wallpaper.**

Choose: You will see Dynamic, Still, and Live galleries in a row with the series of your photo events arranged in the column below.

➤ Tap on any of the Wallpaper options provided or your customized personal photo.

➤ Tap on a Set option below the **Wallpaper**. But, if you do not like it, you may select **Cancel** to take you back to Wallpaper. Choose a page to re-choose wallpaper.

➤ Optional Dialog Box will display three possible options that you may separately consider. There you can choose any of these

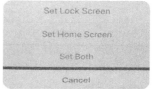

options **Set Home Screen, Set Lock Screen,** or **Set Both.**
Set Home Screen: The Wallpaper you have chosen will only appear on Home Screen.
Set Lock Screen: The Wallpaper will only show on the Lock Screen.
Set Both: The Wallpaper will show on both the Lock Screen and Home Screen. Therefore, you can choose two different Wallpapers for the two screens (i.e. Home & Lock Screens).

Homescreen Smart Tips

The Homescreen clever tips will prevent your iPhone from performing any of these malfunctions such as sudden sluggishness, jacking, irregular response to finger touch, or auto-switch off.

1. Always ensure that all the open pages on your iPhone had been completely closed on your iPhone before you sleep your iPhone.
2. Ensure your iPhone is fully charged before you use it to perform long tasking activities.
3. Set low power mode on your iPhone to reduce the rate of energy consumption when battery capacity is 50 percent or less.
4. When the battery is low, virtually all the animation activation will stop working including the Live Wallpaper you have selected.

How to Launch Lock Screen from the Home Screen

Homescreen to Lock Screen: Swipe down the left side of the Notch of your iPhone, alternatively place a finger at the center of the Notch bottom frame, and swipe down the screen toward the bottom of the iPhone. The Lock Screen will show.

How to Reduce Open Pages into the App icons on the Homescreen

On Homescreen

> Tap on two-three different apps' icons on the Homescreen.
> Place your finger at the bottom center of the screen of the page.
> Slightly move up your finger for a small distance and take off your finger from the screen. You will see the app's page entering the app icon on the Homescreen.

How to See the Reduced Apps' Pages

How to Show the Minimized Pages at the Middle of the Home Screen

> Move up your finger from the bottom center of the iPhone screen and slightly move it in an inverted seven Γ direction.
> As your finger is moving toward the right side of the iPhone you will see those open pages coming out from the left side of the screen.

➢ You can tap on any of the reduced-opened app pages you still want to revisit to work on or get more information from.

How to Show Minimized Pages at the Bottom Center of the Home Screen

➢ Place your finger on the first end of the horizontal Homescreen Bar at the bottom center of the iPhone and move your finger to the second end of the parallel bar.
➢ As you are moving the finger the page will be coming out one after the other. You can move from right to left or vice versa.
➢ Tap on any page you are looking for and it will fully display on the screen of the iPhone.

How to Remove the Minimized Apps' Pages

Page Pressing Down Method (after showing minimized page steps)

➢ When you press down the minimized app's pages one by one for a while, they will show a **Remove Sign** of Minus, a red circle at the left top edge of their pages.
➢ Tap the **Remove** sign to completely delete the reduced page(s).

Swiping Method (after showing minimized page steps)

➢ Place a finger on the individual minimized opened app and further swipe up to completely remove the page from the iPhone.

The complete removal of the reduced opened pages on your iPhone regularly will prevent your iPhone from a drastic slowdown of speed.

How You Can Ensure Low Power Mode Battery Manager

The use of battery mode on your iPhone will enable you to use your averagely charged battery three times longer than normal battery strength.

When you have set the battery mode on your iPhone to be active at a 50% charged level, it will actively reduce many apps that are internally using the battery abnormally. However, the brightness of the screen light will be regulated according to the level of brightness you have set for **Low Power Mode** in the settings.

The Live Wallpaper will stop working when battery mode is active.

Activate Through Settings

On Homescreen: Tap on the **Settings Icon.**

On Settings: Move down the page to tap on **Battery**

On Battery:

> ➢ Tap on the **Low Power Mode** to be activated by changing the button to a Green color.
> ➢ Go back to the Home screen by backing the pages from the top left corner or swiping up from the bottom center of the iPhone.

Activate Through Control Center

You can quickly activate the **Low Power Mode** Manually if you have customized the control through settings.

On Homescreen/Lock Screen: Place your hand at the right side of the Notch above and swipe down to launch **Control Center.**

On Control Center: Tap on **Low Power Mode** icon to activate the feature on the iPhone. The surrounding icon will change to white and the battery charge level will be yellow if it is activated.

How You Can Activate Battery Auto-Lock Control to Improve Battery Life-Time

Auto-lock comes to action immediately after the idle time interval you have set has elapsed. That is, the iPhone will automatically lock itself after the seconds or minutes you have given to your iPhone to be active when you have stopped using it has passed.

In the Settings, you can instruct your iPhone to lock itself at any of this period below or you may even choose "Never" which is not helpful to the iPhone Battery.

➢ 30 Seconds
➢ 1–5 Minutes

On Homescreen: Tap on **Settings Icon.**

On Settings: Gently move down of the page to select **Display & Brightness.**

On Display & Brightness

➢ Tap on the **Brightness** activating switch to change to a Green color.
➢ As you have activated the switch the Brightness regulator will be active. Then Move the Brightness regulator toward the left to reduce the light intensity.

Night Shift: If you have not activated the **Night Shift,** tap on it and put it "ON". After you have activated it, go to the Control center to deactivate it by pressing down the **Screen Light Control** (Brightness control) and tap on **True Tone.**

Auto-Lock: Tap on the Auto-Lock to select your preferred time that you want your iPhone to remain active when you are doing anything.

Rise to Wake: Put "On" the activator, so that you may tap your iPhone screen when it is about to sleep.

Text Size: If you are not satisfied with the font size of the whole text on your iPhone you can go ahead and tap the **Text Size.** Move the Knob regulator toward the right to enlarge the text size on your iPhone screen. But, If, it is already too large, you can then move the knob regulator toward the left to reduce it. (Optional)

Bold Text: You can make all the text on your iPhone screen appear bold if you are not satisfied with the current look of the text font on your iPhone.

Hint: If you alter the text size or bold text, it will surely affect all the words on your iPhone.

CHAPTER FOUR

All the Apps You Can Use to Communicate on Your iPhone XR

The applications (Apps) that have communication features on your iPhone will enable you to pass across information to people that are very essential to you and also receive information from them. The apps will give access to hear the live voice of your communicator(s) or record conversations between them.

More so, through the communication app, you can make live text chat with your dearest fellows or colleagues or business partners or family and instantly receive a reply with the use of cellular data or subscription.

Above all, you can make conference audio or video calls with several people. The Apps that have the **Communication Features** are:

1. Call App
2. FaceTime App
3. Message App
4. Mail App

The Apps that help in getting more information for communication Apps are:

1. Safari App
2. Siri App
3. iTunes App

All You Need to Know About iPhone App

 The call app is one of the most essential primary cores of using the iPhone for communication. The use of the iPhone App will enable you rich-out to your people through their phone numbers.

People's phone numbers could be categorized into two places to separate the most important ones from general ones.

The most important people are considered to be your **Favorites** on the iPhone while others belong to the general **Contacts.** You can assign a separate ringing tone to all contacts in **Favorites.**

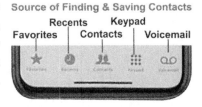

Source of Finding & Saving Contacts

By default, the Phone App is specifically positioned at the base bar of the Homescreen to ease your making and receiving of calls.

To save your friend contact in iPhone app contacts, you will need their phone number, first and last name, email (if available), and picture (if available). But, it is very advisable to save your friend's email in the contact detail because you may need to reach him/her through your Email massage.

Add Contact and Call

On Homescreen: Tap on the **Phone App** at the base bar of your iPhone.

On Favorites

> Tap on the **Favorite** icon (Star) at the bottom left of the screen.
> Tap on **Add** icon (Cross) at the top left of your iPhone's screen.
> Go through all contact to locate the named contact or enter the name of the person into the **Search field** to quickly see the **Person's Contact.**
> Tap on the Contact Name
  Optional Dialog Box: Tap on the usual way of contacting people such as Message (iMessage or Mail), Call, or FaceTime. For example, select Call.
  Immediately, you will see the selected contact name among **Favorites.**

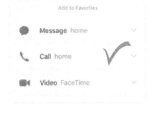

69

OR

On Homescreen: Tap on the **Phone App** at the base bar of your iPhone.

On Contacts

> Tap on **Contacts Icon** at the bottom center of the iPhone's screen.
> Tap on the **search field** to quickly locate the contact's name you are looking for.
> Tap on the contact's name to see all the person's information details, below you will see **Add to Favorites.**
> Tap on the Contact Name
> **Optional Dialog Box:** Tap on the usual way of contacting people such as Message (iMessage or Mail), Call, or FaceTime. For example, select Call.
> Immediately, you will see the selected contact name among **Favorites.**

Remove a Contact from Your iPhone

You need to understand the fact that, whenever you apply to **Delete** command on any contact on your iPhone or Email account, it will completely remove it from your iPhone without a chance of retrieving/restoring it.

Therefore, you have to be sure about the contact before you tap on the **Delete** command.

On Homescreen: Tap on **Contacts Icon**

On Contacts

> Search for the **Contact's Name** through the search field
> Tap on the exact **Contacts Name**
> Tap on **Edit**
> Move down the screen to tap on **Delete Contacts.**

70

> For confirmation re-tap on **Delete Contacts** (Confirmatory Dialog Box**)**. Immediately the contact will be completely removed from your iPhone Contacts list.

Set Sorting Order of Contacts List on Your iPhone

The Names of everyone in your Contacts could be arranged in a chronological order from A-Z to ease the searching of either **First or Second Name.**

You are given the privilege to instruct your iPhone on how you want the name to be arranged, that is if you want the First name to appear before the second the following setting will enable it:

On Homescreen: Tap on the **Settings Icon**

On Settings: Scroll down to select **Contacts**

On Contacts

> **Sort Order:** This will alphabetically arrange either the First or Second Name in Contacts.
> **Display Order**: This will either display the First Name after or before Second Name.

Short Name: Select how the Contact's Name will show in your iPhone, Mail, Messages, FaceTime... and other Apps.

Move Contacts from SIM to iPhone

You can transfer all your contacts on your SIM into your new iPhone if the SIM supports the feature. It is very easy to do.

SIM Card Insertion: Insert your SIM containing the contacts you want to transfer into your iPhone.

On Homescreen: Tap on the **Settings Icon**

On Settings: Tap on **Contacts**

On Contacts:

- ➢ Move to the middle of the screen to tap on **Import SIM Contacts.**
- ➢ Tap where the contacts should be imported from an optional dialog box that will appear.
- ➢ Hold on till the whole contacts moving process is finished before you proceed.
- ➢ Access your Contact to confirm the complete importation on your iPhone.

Hints: iPhone cannot save the contact(s) on SIM card, if you want to transfer contacts from iPhone to iPhone then there will be a need for you to back up the iPhone with iCloud storage or other transferring means like PC memory, flash, etc.

Activate and Deactivate Contacts for Mail Account

The activation of Contacts will enable you to add contacts in any of your Email Account and deactivation of Contacts will enable the removal of contact(s) from your iPhone.

On Homescreen: Tap **Settings Icon**

On Settings: Tap on **Password and Account**

On Password and Account: Tap on the **Email Account.**

On The Email Account (Gmail/Yahoo): Switch On the **Contacts Activator** to become Green.

To Deactivate Contacts App

The Email Account (Gmail/Yahoo)

- ➢ Switch Off the **Contacts Activator** to become **White.**
- ➢ Tap **Delete from My iPhone.** Immediately the contact will be removed.

Make Your Contacts for Email Account

On Homescreen: Tap on **Settings Icon**

On Settings: Tap on **Password and Account**

On Password and Account: Tap on **Add Account**

On Add Account: Tap on your Email account and switch On **Contacts.**

If you do not have an email account you can tap on **Other** to make Contact Accounts such as LDAP or CardDAV account.

> ➢ Type your details and password.
> ➢ Tap on **Next.**

In a situation whereby you are having several accounts set up in the Contacts App and you need a particular account for the contacts: Do this;

On Homescreen: Tap on **Contacts** App

On Contacts: Tap **Groups** at the top left angle of the screen.

Add New Contact to Your Default Account

This is very advisable for you if you are using more than one Email Account in your **Contacts.**

On Homescreen: Tap on **Settings Icon**

On Settings: Scroll down to select **Contacts**

On Contacts: tap on **Default Account**

On Default Account: Select **One** of your **Email Accounts.**

How You Can Make A Call Conveniently

On Homescreen: Tap on **Phone App**

Keypad Interface

> ➢ Type the **Contact Number** on the

73

Keypad if you do not have the person's contact in your iPhone **Contact List.**

➤ Tap on the **Call Button.** It is the Green Circle.

End Call

➤ The Green Circle Button will change to Red Circle Button, it is called the **End Button.**
➤ Tap the **End Button** to stop the call.

Make A Call from Contacts

Keypad Interface: Look at the bottom center to tap on **Contacts.**

Contacts:

➤ Enter the first two alphabetical letters that started the name of the person into the search field to speed up the quick discovery of the contact.
➤ Tap on the **Contact's Name**

Contact's Name: Tap on the person's Phone Number.

End Call: Tap on the **End Button** to stop the call.

Add People's Phone Number to Your Contact Directly

Keypad Interface

➤ Dial the **Phone Number** of the person correctly.
➤ Tap on **Add to Contact** at the top of the screen.

Request Dialog Box: On a displayed **Request Dialog Box** tap **Create New Contact.**

Create New Contact

➤ Type the First and Second Name of the person

- ➢ Enter the Email of the owner of the Phone Number if you know it (optional).
- ➢ You can choose different **Ringtones** for the contact (optional).
- ➢ Tap on **Add to Existing Contact**

Add to Existing Contact

- ➢ Look for the **Contact**
- ➢ Enter the Number into the Number text field
- ➢ Tap on **Done.**

Add To Contacts from Recent Called or Received Contacts

You can add the recently ended call phone number into your general Contact by following these steps on your iPhone.

Keypad Interface: Look below and tap **Recents** with a round clock icon.

Recent

- ➢ You will see the recently ended phone number
- ➢ Tap on the **Info icon** in front of the phone number.

Info: Select **Create New Contact**

Create New Contact

- ➢ Type the First and Second Names
- ➢ Enter the Email of the owner of the Phone Number if you know it (optional).
- ➢ You can choose different **Ringtones** for the contact it is optional.
- ➢ Tap on **Add to Existing Contact**

Add to Existing Contact

- ➢ Look for the **Contact**
- ➢ Enter the Number into the Number text field
- ➢ Tap on **Done.**

Now the recent call will appear with the name you used to add the number into your Contact. The person contact can be found in your overall **Contact list** on your iPhone.

How to Delete all Recent Contacts

A recent list comprises the phone numbers of all those you have called, received calls and missed incoming calls, and missed outgoing calls with the day and time they were called or received. You can easily remove all the recent history.

On Homescreen: Tap on **Phone App Icon**

Keypad Interface: look at the bottom left of the screen and tap on **Recents** (Round Clock Icon).

Recent

- ➢ Look at the top left of the screen tap on **Clear**
- ➢ Tap on the **Clear All Recents** button showing down the screen. If you tap the **Cancel** button, it will reverse the action and the recent list will not be deleted.

What You Can Do When You Are on a Call

1. You can switch it to outside **Speaker**
2. You can switch to Video Call.
3. You can allow more people to participate in your discussion.
4. You can Mute the Voice.
5. You can Accept or Decline other incoming calls.
6. You can compose a message to reply to your call.
7. You can make use of Remind Me as a remainder to later return the call of the caller.
8. You can search through apps (e.g. Mail, Photo, Note, Calendar, Safari, Social Media) to get relevant information. Browsing Apps will require a Wi-Fi network connection on your iPhone.

How to Allow or Prevent Call When You Are On A Call

To Accept Call: On the calling, the interface slides the Call button toward the right to answer the call.

To Prevent the Call and Forward It into Voicemail: Double-click the **Power Button** at the right side of the iPhone.

Send Message To Caller: Tap on the **Message Icon** to text messages and send them to your caller.

Use Reminder To Recall: You can tap on the **Remind Me** to remind you to call the caller after you stop the current call.

How You Can Make Your Voicemail Active

 Voicemail has a feature that can play your recorded voice greeting to tell the reason why you are not available to receive calls at the moment and also record and play the voice of the caller that audibly delivered messages for a very short time for you to hear.

You can also choose a greeting out of some default recorded greetings for your outgoing greeting.

To make Voicemail active, you have to go into the Setting or through Voicemail Icon in the Phone app to Set Up your **Password and Greeting**.

On Homescreen: Tap on the **Phone App** icon.

On Keypad Interface: Below the screen tap on **Voicemail Icon** at the last bottom left.

Voicemail: Tap on **Set Up Now.**

Password

> ➢ Type in the **Voicemail Password** that must be in 4-digit.
> ➢ Retype the same **Voicemail Password** to confirm your consistency.

> ➤ Tap on **Custom** options to make your outgoing greeting with your voice or otherwise.
> ➤ Tap on **Record** to start. (Say your greeting as you want it to be said).
> ➤ Tap on **Stop** to end the recording.
> ➤ Tap on **Play** to hear your recorded greeting.
> ➤ If you are not okay, you can re-tap the **Record.**
> ➤ If you are okay then tap on **Save**

How to Reset Voicemail Set Up Through Settings

On Homescreen: Tap on the **Settings icon.**

On Settings: Select **Phone App**

On Phone: Tap on **Change Voicemail Password**

Password

> ➤ Tap on **New Password**
> ➤ Type in the **Previous Password**
> ➤ Type in the **New Password**
> ➤ Tap on **Done.**

How to Listen to Your Voicemail

 If you are having calls that have been forwarded into Voicemail, you will see the notification number of new Voicemails at the top-right edge side of the **Voicemail Icon** and the last bottom left of the keypad interface.

On Homescreen: Tap on the **Phone App** icon.

Keypad Interface: Below the screen tap on the **Voicemail Icon** at the last bottom left.

Voicemail

78

- ➢ Tap on the **Message**
- ➢ Tap on **Play** to hear the recorded caller's voice.
- ➢ Tap on **Call Back** to replay the voice message.
- ➢ If you are satisfied with the message you can tap on Delete.

To Call the Voicemail caller

On Homescreen: Tap on the **Phone App** icon.

Keypad Interface: Below the screen tap on **Voicemail Icon** at the last bottom left.

Voicemail:

- ➢ Tap on **Call Voicemail.**
- ➢ Tap on the **End Button.**

Send Junk and Unwanted Callers into Voicemail

This will only allow the saved contacts on your iPhone to ring out but unknown contacts will be sent to Voicemail

On Homescreen: Tap on the **Settings icon.**

On Settings: Tap on **Phone**

Phone: Tap on the **Silence Unknown Caller** activator to become Green.

Set Call Waiting in Settings

Wi-Fi Network connection is very important to make Wi-Fi call active in Dual SIM. You will see Call Waiting when one line call is active and another incoming call occurs in another line.

On Homescreen: Tap on **Settings**

On Settings: Tap on **Phone App**

On Phone: Select **Call Waiting** and tap on the activator to become Green.

- ➢ Make Home Swipe Up

How to Set Special Ringtones for Calls, Messages, Alert, & Mail Notifications

You can set separate ringtones to different contacts in iPhone Contacts. You may consider giving a similar ringtone and vibration to all the contacts in your Favorite and different ringtones to some set of people in all Contacts.

You can use a special ringtone to know when your close family members in the Favorites are calling and when your important business partners are calling.

On Homescreen: Tap on **Settings**

On Settings: Tap on **Sound & Hepatics**

On Sound & Hepatics

- ➢ Tap on the **Vibrate on Ring** activator to turn Green
- ➢ Tap on the **Vibrate on Silence** activator to turn Green
- ➢ Select your **Ringtone** and choose any of the default Ringtones available.

How to Set a Specific Ringtone for Individual Contact

On Homescreen: Tap on the **Contact App** icon

On Contacts

- ➢ Search for contact through the search field.
- ➢ Tap on the **Contact**
- ➢ Tap on **Edit**
- ➢ Tap on **Ringtone**
- ➢ Select one of the **Default Ringtones**.
- ➢ Make **Home Swipe Up**.

CHAPTER FIVE

The Complete Benefit of FaceTime App on Your iPhone XR

 FaceTime App is a loving video method that can be used to communicate with other iPhone users or those iPhone users on your iPhone Contacts.

It has a unique video communication feature that can allow you to see the face of the person you are calling or the person that called you.

Most of the time, it is important that you first send a *video call request* to the person you want to make a FaceTime call with on either interactive iMessages interface or through an audio call that you will like to make or switch to FaceTime Video Call.

You have to ensure that the person you are trying to call with the FaceTime app is using iPhone and you are having enough Wi-Fi Data to make the call.

You can also use FaceTime to make Conference Video Call with other iPhone users in your contacts but you must notify those that will participate in the conference call through text message. Notifying them why you are about to have a group discussion, and ask each of them if they will be available.

Make FaceTime Set Up in Settings to be Active

On Homescreen: Tap on the **Settings Icon**

On Settings: Scroll down to select **FaceTime**

On FaceTime

- ➢ Turn On the **FaceTime** Activator to become Green
- ➢ Turn On the **FaceTime Live Photo** Activator to become Green

81

- ➢ Provide your **Phone Number**
- ➢ Provide your **Apple ID**
- ➢ Provide your **Email Add** (Optional)

Make FaceTime Audio Calls or Video Call

On Homescreen: Tap on the **FaceTime Icon**

On FaceTime: Tap on the **Add Contact** at the top right corner of the screen.

On Contact: Use the search field to quickly get the contact.

Audio Call: Tap on the **Audio Call button** to fix the audio call.

OR

Video Call: Tap on the **Video Call button** to fix the video call.

How to Change from Normal Audio Calls to FaceTime Video Call

On the calling interface, you will see an option of using FaceTime Video

Video Call: Tap on the **Video Call button** to fix a video call.

Tap on the **End button** at the lower left of the FaceTime Video call interface. ⊗

How You Can Change from Text Message Interaction to FaceTime Call

On Homescreen: Tap on **Messages App Icon**

Message

> Tap on the **Compose icon** at the top right of the screen.

> Type the name of the person you want to chat within the "**To**" Search field.
> During the live iMessage chatting with your friend, hit on the name of your friend at the top center of the screen to choose FaceTime.
> Tap on **FaceTime Icon**
> Choose either **Audio or Video Call**
> Tap on the **End button** to end the FaceTime call

How to Make Multiple Live Chat

On Homescreen: Tap on the **Messages App Icon**

On Messages

> Tap on the **Compose icon** at the top right of the screen.

> Type the **Names or Phone Number or Email Add** of all persons you want to chat with into the "**To**" Search field. For example, *Hannah Berm, Daniel Rose, Dan Floral*
> Below the screen tap the text message field for **Keyboard** to show up, type your text message, and tap on **Send icon**

to deliver your message into the chat interface.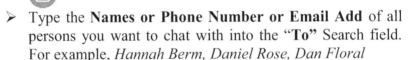

How to Change the Group Conversation to FaceTime Video Call

Use the same step of moving from a single chat to change your communication mode to FaceTime Video or Audio Call.

On Message (Chatting Page)

> Tap on the names of your friends at the top center of the screen to choose **FaceTime**.
> Tap on the **FaceTime Icon**
> Choose either **Audio or Video Call**
> Tap on the **End button** to end the FaceTime call

How to Replace Your Face with Animoji during FaceTime Video

On Homescreen: Launch **FaceTime** App

FaceTime

- ➢ On the FaceTime Call interface tap on the **Video Call button.**
- ➢ Tap on **Effect Button.**
- ➢ Tap on either **Memoji** or **Animoji** available
- ➢ Scroll toward the right or left to choose.
- ➢ Tap on your preferred Memoji or Animoji. Immediately your face will be replaced with chosen Memoji or Animoji.
- ➢ To remove the Memoji or Animoji tap on **Cancel** ✕ and your face reappear normally.

If you want to change the current Memoji or Animoji: Restart all over from the beginning of the above steps and reselect the new Memoji of Animoji of your choice.

The Additional Uses of Message App

You can majorly use the Message App to make a direct live chat with those who are in your iPhone contacts using iMessage.

Also, you can use it to send a text message to those who are in your contacts using Android.

How to Compose and Reply Text Messages

On Homescreen: Tap on **Messages App Icon**

On Messages

- ➢ Tap on the **Compose icon** at the upper right of the screen.
- ➢ Type the name of the person you want to chat with into the "**To**" Search field.
  OR

- ➢ If you want to reply to any received message in the massage App, tap on the particular message. It will launch you into the compose text message interface.
- ➢ Tap on the text field to type your text message.
- ➢ Tap on the **Send Button,** that is, the Blue Send Button is for iMessage ⬆ while Green Send Button is for SMS ⬆.

Your iPhone will automatically determine if the text message is iMessage or SMS. Once you see the blue button showing before you send your text message, that implies you are about to send iMessage to the person using iPhone, but if it shows green that means, you are sending text SMS to an Android user.

How to add Emoji to your Text Message

On Messages

- ➢ At the lower left side of the Keyboard tap on **Emoji** Icon
- ➢ You may scroll up and down or right side to select by tapping on anyone you like.
- ➢ Tap on the Send button to move it into the chat interface.

How to add Effects to your Text Message

Messages

- ➢ At the immediate left side of the Keyboard Text Field, you will see **App Store** Icon, tap on it.
- ➢ Select the **Animoji icon** at the bottom roll menu. 🐶
- ➢ You will see different **Animoji** images.
- ➢ Select Animoji you like and it will be positioned within the focus.

Bring Your Face Into View

Mimicking Your Face & Mouth

> Square view guide. Once the Animoji is balanced, it will be mimicking your face and mouth movement.
> Tap on the **Recording Button** at the lower right side of the view frame to start recording your audio voice with Animoji.
> Tap on the same button to stop the recording and change the button to the **Send** button. It will replay itself for you to hear.

> If you are satisfied then tap on the **Send button** to forward the Animoji into the **Chat** interface for the person you are chatting with to receive and access it.
> You can still reselect another Animoji below by scrolling through the arranged Animoji drawer and tap on another different Animoji to make a new recording.
> If you are not satisfied tap on the **Delete** button at the upper right.

For Additional Effects

> You can still go ahead to get more Animoji in the App Store by tapping on the **App Store** icon at the lower-left corner of the screen and tap on **View Apps.**
> You can still search for "**Images**" that are very accurate to your message by tapping on the **Search Icon** below.
> Tap on the **Find Images Field** showing above the displayed images.
> Enter the types of images you are looking for like Thinking, Disagreement, Excitement, Sleeping, Busy, Hungry, Disturbed, Listening, Working… and many others.

86

You may pick from the appearing keywords as you are entering the word.

➢ There is also a **Free Hand Drawing icon** that could allow you to draw anything you like and send it to the person you are chatting with.

➢ You can also send home videos through **YouTube, Audio Music, Recents Selfie Pictures/other Pictures, or Video** through Camera.

How You Can Make Your Own Animoji or Memoji on Your iPhone XR

On Messages

➢ At the immediate left side of the Keyboard Text Field, you will see **App Store** Icon, tap on it.

➢ Select the **Animoji icon** at the bottom roll menu .

➢ Scroll toward right tap on Add/Cross Sign for **New Memoji**

➢ Select **Skin** and adjust it with the available set of colors and remove face spots by choosing freckles.

➢ Select **Hairstyle** to choose either male hairstyle or female hairstyle.

➢ Move to **Head Shape** to select the loveliest chin.

➢ Move to the **Eye** section to pick the type of eye you like having on your Memoji.

➢ Continue to select all the parts of the face of your Memoji from the other options including **eyebrow, Nose & Lips, Ear** with different pretty earing, **Facial Hair** with either Mustard & Beard or Sideburns, **Eyewear** like glasses, and **Headwear** like face-caps, hat, etc., till you complete achieve a beautiful looking Memoji. It is a creative place that is full of fun.

➢ As soon as you are satisfied with your **Self Making Memoji** then tap on **Done** to save the Memoji and include it with the group of Animoji.

You can use your Memoji to make FaceTime video calls or iMessage audio chat on the Message App interface of your iPhone.

How to Add Animation Effect to Your Text Message

On Messages

> ➢ Type your short text message into the text field. For example, *Stay Home Safe, Drink Responsibly, Daily Exercise Importance, Let's Jubilate, Today's Plan, etc.*
> ➢ Press and hold the **Send** button for a while to launch the **Effect Page**. This contains:
>> ✓ **Bubble Animation Effects:** Slam, Loud, Gentle and Invisible Ink.
>> ✓ **Screen Animation Effects:** Send with Echo, Send with Confetti, Send with Spotlight... and others.

Send with Effect

> ➢ At the upper center of the page, you will see **Bubble & Screen.**
> ➢ Tap one of the various effects menus to know the best. Once you have known the best effect, leave it on the option.
> ➢ Tap on the **Screen** option above.
> ➢ Swipe the screen from right to left to see the various screen effects. When you have seen the most suitable **Screen Effect** for your Text message then tap on the **Send** ✖ button.
> ➢ If you are not satisfied then tap on the **Cancel** button to return to the message interface.

How to Send Voice Message

This makes the message easy for those who are not having enough time to chat with a text message or those who are not very fast in typing text messages to quickly deliver their messages, as a result, they can choose a short audio recording message that is précised, specific, and fast.

On Messages

88

- ➤ Go to the bottom left of the keyboard and tap on the **Microphone Icon.**
- ➤ Start an audio message. You will see the linear sound wave of your voice as you are talking. The louder your voice the bigger the size of the sound wave.
- ➤ As soon as you finished the audio message, tap **Send** button above.
- ➤ It will be seen in the chat interface.
- ➤ Look at the bottom left of the screen and tap on the Keyboard icon to return to the Keyboard.

Hint: You can also dictate your message to Siri that is capable of changing all your audio dictation messages to text messages and sending them to the right contact.

Things You Can Use Mail App For

Mail app is an avenue to receive and send a message(s) with the use of Electronic Mail (Email) Service Providers which include **Google** (...@gmail.com), **Yahoo** (...@ yahoo.com), **iCloud** (...@icloud.com), **Outlook.com** (...@outlook.com)... and many others.

The use of the Mail App will fully allow you to receive or send documents to loved ones and business associates. It is more officially used for a better transaction between you and other business organizations.

Mail has become the most reliable acceptable official interactive platform to provide you with vital details and effectively perform online obligations.

There are channels through which you can get information in which you can add your composed message. Such an addition is called **Document Attachment.**

You can save documents with any **Microsoft Office** format or you may directly go to a website to copy very relevant information that is helpful to clarify your message and subsequently paste it within your message.

If you are already having two or more email accounts and you want to add them to your new iPhone there are some simple steps you have to take in your iPhone Account Settings.

To make Mail effectively functional, then you have to carry out either the manual or automatic setup in Settings on your iPhone.

How to Manually Set Up Mail

The manual setup is simply designed for those who are using different Emails from the usual email accounts that are suggested on the Add Account Interface. Then, the **Other** is the correct option to choose.

On Homescreen: tap on the **Settings** icon.

On Settings: Move down and select **Accounts & Passwords.**

On Accounts & Passwords: Tap on the **Add Account**

On Add Account: Look at the lower part of the screen and tap on **Other.**

On Other: Tap on the **Add Mail Account**

New Account

> ➢ Type your **Name**
> ➢ Type your specific **Email**

90

Account

➢ Type your **Password**
➢ Type your **Description**
➢ Tap on **Next** for the setup to be finalized and the Mail will search for your Email Account.
➢ Once the searching is successful then tap on **Done.**

If the Email Account settings could not be found then do the following to round up the setup.

Second Phase New Account: If you do not know your Email settings ask your email service provider to tell you if the email settings belong to IMAP or POP. As soon as you have confirmed this, do the following:

➢ Tap on **IMAP/POP**
➢ Provide details on **INCOMING & OUTCOMING MAIL SERVER**
  ✓ **Host Name**
  ✓ **User Name & Password**
➢ Tap on **Next** at the top.
➢ Once your details are accurate then tap on **Save**

Your inability to provide the correct details will lead to the inability to complete the manual setup.

How to Put Automatic Set Up for Mail App in Place

On Homescreen: Tap on the **Settings** icon.

On Settings: Scroll down and select **Accounts & Passwords.**

On Accounts & Passwords: Tap on the **Add Account**

91

On Add Account: Select your Email service source (e.g. Yahoo).

Yahoo

> Type your existing **Yahoo Address**
> Type correct **Password**

(If you want to look into your email account then you can tap on **Sign In**, when you are done, then **Sign Out** to return to the previous Set Up page because you still have some tasks to complete. Better still, complete the tasks before you Sign-In in to your account).

> Tap on **Next** to continue and hold on for the processing to complete.

In Your Yahoo Account (...@yahoo.com)

> Switch On the **Activator** ⬤ of the following applications **Contacts App, Mail Contacts, Calendar App, Note App** & **Reminder App.**
> At the upper right region of the screen tap on **Save.**

How to Activate the Function of Essential Tools for Message Composition

All essential tools for a perfect write-up and excellent message composition should be activated in the Settings to ensure correct spellings, arrangement, capitalization... and many others.

On Homescreen: Tap on the **Settings icon**

On Settings: Select **General**

General: Select **Keyboards**

On Keyboards: Switch On the following **Activation buttons** ⬤ of **Auto-Capitalization, Auto-Correction, Check Spelling, Enable Caps Lock, Predictive, Smart Punctuation, Character Preview, Shortcut, and Enable Dictation.**

To Change Your Keyboard to One-Handed Keyboard

On the same Keyboards page

Keyboards: Select **One-Handed Keyboard** and tap on the **Activator**

OR

You can also get the selection of One-Handed Keyboard directly on the Mail to compose page.

On Homescreen: Tap on **Mail App**

On Mail: Tap the **Compose icon** at the top right region of the screen or select received Email and later tap on compose or reply icon. ☑️

On New Message

> ➤ Tap the front of "**To:**" for the text cursor to show and the Keyboard to show below.
> ➤ At the lower region of the Keyboard in the new message interface, press down the Earth icon 🌐 for different types of Keyboard to show.
> ➤ Tap on either the left or right-hand side Keyboard that is very convenient for you.

How to Write and Send Email Messages

Homescreen: First and foremost, go to the **Control Center** to put On Wi-Fi Network and tap on **Mail App**

Mail: Tap Compose Icon at the top right region of the screen or select received Email and later tap on compose or reply icon. ☑️

New Message

- Tap the front of "**To:**" for the text cursor to show and the Keyboard to show below.
- Type the **Name or Email Address** of the receiving contact (the person's or company's email address).
- Tap the front of "**Subject:**" to type a short theme of your message.
- Tap on the text field interface to start writing your text message. Once you are through then tap on the **Send icon** at the top right region of the screen ⬆.
- How to Directly Get Name or Email from Your iPhone Contact.

You can directly get the name or email address of the person you want to send an email message to through the Contacts on your iPhone.

New Message: Tap on the **Add/Cross** icon to launch Contacts and use the search field to quickly locate the contact you are looking for.

How to Attach Document to Your Message

It is advisable to attach PDF or JPEG documents to your Email because the document cannot be altered.

Mail: Tap Compose Icon at the top right region of the screen or select received Email and later tap on compose or reply icon. ✉

New Message: After you have entered the above "**To**" info (name or email add of where you are sending a message)**, Subject and** You have composed your message.

- Press down anywhere on the message field for **Edit Menu** to show.
- Tap on the **Arrow** at the end of the **Edit menu** to select **Add Attachment.**

➤ It will open to your iPhone document storage and iCloud Drive. Navigate through the App you used such as **Pages App, Keynotes App...** and others.

For Photo or Video

➤ You can also attach pictures to your message by tapping or pressing down the field and continue to tap on the arrow at the end till you see **Insert Photo** or **Video.**

    ✓ It will launch out your Photo library to select your **Pictures.** Carefully navigate through the exact category you have your pictures.

    ✓ Tap on your **Pictures** and **Send** them to upload on your massage field.

Copy Information from Website

    ✓ At the down middle of the iPhone Notch, slide down a little to see the App browsing text field.

    ✓ Enter Safari, you will see the App and tap on it to access the web page.

    ✓ Enter web add, highlight the massage, and tap copy.

    ✓ Go to the base of the horizontal bar and swipe from the left end to the right end. You will see the New Message page.

    ✓ Tap the place you want to paste the copied info to display on the message field for the edit menu to show an option of **Paste.** Tap Paste and what you copied will display.

OR

    Homescreen: Tap on Safari to launch the web add text field.

    ✓ Copy your message as explained above.

    ✓ Move your finger from the middle bottom of the iPhone in inverted seven ⌐ to see the minimized **New Message Page**.

    ✓ Tap on the New Message Page and follow the above-pasting steps.

➤ Once you are through with all the documents attachment, then tap on **Send** .

All You Can Ask Siri Through Voice Dictation

Siri features will help you to organize and properly program your hourly, daily, weekly, monthly, and yearly activities successfully.

It is a unique dictating tool in iPhone that can help you to easily operate all the applications on your iPhone quickly. Siri can help you activate any app or control on your iPhone.

Siri can give you the current information happening around the world; it could tell you the climatic condition at any time, traffic condition, and remind you of every important saved event in your organizer or calendar.

Siri could help you set an alarm when you ask it to do so. It can change your dictated message to a text message and send it to the instructed contact. It can translate the English language to any other language like French, German, Spanish... and more others.

It can help you locate a place on a Google map and show you the bearing compass to get to the place. It can assist you to find out a review or reputation about an organization or person.

Siri can tell you where you can locate your favorite contacts on your iPhone that you have already registered with Siri. It could help you forward calls to your acquainted favorites or anyone in your contact... and many other benefits.

When you call Siri, you will hear a human voice that could be a female or male voice. It depends on the voice of whom you have selected in the Siri Settings.

However, for you to know all that Siri could do on your iPhone, follow the information in the next subtopic.

How You Can Effectively Make Siri Serve You

For Siri to work on your iPhone efficiently, you must first finish the setup in the settings, if you have not done it during the iPhone Automatic Setup or Manual Setup.

On Homescreen: Tap on **Settings**

On Settings: Scroll down to select **Siri & Search**

Siri & Search: Turn On all the below **Activation Buttons** and select your preferable features for each option.

- ➤ Listen for "Hey Siri".
- ➤ Press Side Button for Siri.
- ➤ Allow Siri When Locked.
- ➤ Language.
- ➤ Siri Voice.
- ➤ Voice Feedback.
- ➤ My Information.
- ➤ **SIRI SUGGESTIONS**
  - ✓ Suggestion in Search
  - ✓ Suggestions in Lock Up

On Lock Screen or Homescreen:

- ➤ Unlock the iPhone (If you did not activate " When Locked")
- ➤ Press the Switch, Sleep, or Wake Button on the right side of your iPhone. (If you have activated "Press Side Button for Siri")
- ➤ **Say** Hey Siri! What can Siri do
- ➤ Siri will respond and show you all things that it could do.

You can also use Apple Earpods to call the attention of Siri

- ➤ Click the Answering middle button to call Siri's attention.

Without Clicking on Side Button on Homescreen,

- ➤ Say Hey Siri!
- ➤ Immediately Siri will answer you. Siri is very sensitive to "Hey Siri", and then continue with your question.

How You Can Perfectly Use Safari App

 In your iPhone, Safari App makes use of Cellular Service and Wi-Fi Network Data to facilitate its function and efficiency. However, without Cellular Service and Wi-Fi network data, you cannot make use of the Safari App

The use of the Safari app will give you the privilege to visit many websites and move from a webpage to another webpage to gather several details or facts online.

Safari suggests a more related website that you can get more useful information and also display all your favorite websites.

You can download or save apps through the Safari browser on your iPhone into My iPhone File or iCloud drive. The Safari browsing window is loaded with many beneficial tools like:

- ➤ **Page Icon:** To move from one webpage to another webpage ⬜
  - ✓ **Add New Tab (Add Icon ⊹)** to add more Tab
  - ✓ **Private** to open a confidential browsing window.
  - ✓ **Close Icon** to delete the page at the top left edge ✗
  - ✓ **Done**
- ➤ **Share Icon** to send a page to other apps like Mail, Message, Add to Notes, Bookmark, Reading List, etc.; or to social media page which will be displayed among the options of where you can save the webpage. Check any of the below options to determine what format the document will be sent:

- ✓ **Automatic:** It will select the exact appropriate format for every application or action
- ✓ **PDF**
- ✓ **Web Archive**
- ➤ **Download Icon** to access the recent download files on Safari. ⬇
- ➤ **URL with A Small and A Big (AA):** Small A is used to reduce the font size and the big A is to increase the font size. It is designed to enable the following settings:
  - ✓ Small A Font Size Settings
  - ✓ Big A Size Settings
  - ✓ Show Reader View
  - ✓ Hide Toolbar
  - ✓ Request Desktop Website
  - ✓ Website Settings ⊘

How to Activate/Enable the Safari Settings

On Homepage: Tap on **Settings**.

On Settings: Scroll down the screen and tap on **Safari**

On Safari

- ➤ **SEARCH**
  Allow Safari to access Siri by tapping on **Siri & Search** and Activate the switch.
- ➤ **SEARCH**
  - ✓ **Search Engine** will select your preferable source e.g. Google.
  - ✓ Put On the **Searching Engine Suggestions** Activator.
  - ✓ Put On the **Safari Suggestions** Activator.
  - ✓ Tap on **Quick Website Search** to select **On**
  - ✓ Put On the **Preload Top Tap** Activator.
- ➤ **GENERAL**
  - ✓ Activate **Autofill**

- ✓ Turn On the **Frequency Visited Sites** Activator.

- ✓ Turn On the **Favorite** Activator
- ✓ Tap on **Favorites** to select **Favorites**
- ✓ Turn On the **Block Pop-up** Activator
- ✓ Turn On the **Show Link Previews** Activator
- ✓ Tap on **Download** to select the storage source e.g. My iPhone and iCloud.

➤ **TABS**
- ✓ Turn On **Show Tab Bar** Activator
- ✓ If you want Icons to be shown in the Tab then you may put On **Show Icons in Tabs'** activation button.
- ✓ Tap on **Open Links** to select **In New Tab**
- ✓ Tap on **Close Tabs** to select when you want the open tabs to be closed automatically by Safari. (e.g. Manually, After One Day, After One Week or After One Month).

➤ **PRIVACY & SECURITY**
- ✓ Turn On **Prevent Cross-Site Tracking** activator.

- ✓ Do not activate **Block All Cookies** because they cannot transmit viruses and your iPhone details cannot be hacked by network hackers.
- ✓ Turn On **Fraudulent Websites Warning**'s activator
- ✓ Turn On **Check for Apple Pay** activator: it will enable you to make use of Apple Pay if you are having an Apple Account and Apple Pay is activated in the Siri settings.

➤ **Clear History and Website Data:** If you tap this option you will be able to clear all the browsing history and website data on your iPhone.

➤ **SETTING FOR WEBSITE**
- ✓ Tap on **Page Zoom** for selection between 50%-300% but you may choose 100% for the normal setting.

100

- ✓ Tap on **Request Desktop Website** for selection of Websites.
- ✓ Tap on **Reader** for selection
- ✓ Tap on **Camera** for selection of Image Size.
- ✓ Tap on **Microphone** for selection

➢ **READING LIST**
   - ✓ You can activate the **Automatically Save Offline** if you want all reading lists in the iCloud to be automatically saved.
   - ✓ Tap on **Advance** for selection.

How To Start Safari Browsing Benefit on Your iPhone

On Homescreen: Tap on **Safari Icon** at the lower bar menu of the page.

On Safari:

➢ Tap on the **Browsing Text Field** to type in your searching words from the appeared keyboard.
   - ✓ You may select from the predictive dropdown keywords.
   - ✓ You may also type your web address directly if you are very sure about it.

➢ Tap on the **"Go"** button on your keyboard and what you are looking for will come up.

If you are searching for social media applications like Facebook, WhatsApp... and many others then tap on the app or tap on the download option if you want to download on your iPhone.

For **Webpage**: Once the page displays "you want to save the page as **Bookmark** for future or reference purpose":
   - ✓ Tap on **Bookmark Icon** at the bottom of the page.

   📖

   - ✓ Select **Add Bookmark for 3 Tabs** on the informative dialog box to **Save** it inside a **New Folder**.

✓ **New Folder:** Give the **Web Tab** a Name, tap on **Done** and it will be saved in the Favorite browsing tabs.

✓ If you want to open the web tab later. Tap on Bookmark and select the Name of the web tab and the page will open.

➢ **About Favorites:** These are the websites that you have visited often and they will be automatically displayed below your Safari browsing search field.

✓ You can just tap on any of the web icons to directly launch the webpage of the website without you retyping the website address into the search field machine.

✓ It is very easy and pretty cool to use.

✓ If you still want to open another website, all you need to do is to tap on **Add New Tab** Icon at the right bottom side of the screen. ⊥

✓ A new page with your favorite websites will be displayed then tap on the other website to also launch another webpage easily.

➢ **Move From Tab Page To Another Tab Page**

✓ Tap on the **Switch Page Icon** ▢ at the last right bottom of the screen.

✓ You will see all the open pages filed up behind one another. With the help of your finger slightly swipe down to reselect any of the pages by tapping on the page.

✓ **Delete Tab Page:** Look at the top left edge of each page you will see **Cancel Icon**, tap on it and the tab page will be deleted.

➢ **Other Places You Can Save Your Page** ⬆

✓ Tap on the **Share Icon** to access the various apps that you can choose and save the web page, as I have mentioned above.

➢ **Use Share Icon to Transfer Webpage from Your iPhone to Another Apple Device** ⬆

- ✓ Go to the bottom of the page and tap on the **Share icon.**
- ✓ Select on **AirDrop** Icon
- ✓ Locate the Apple device **Name** and select. On the other Apple device tap **Accept** on the informative dialog box; instantly you will see the **Webpage** on the other Apple device screen.

What You Can Do When Webpage Is Not Loading on Safari or Safari Is Not Responding

There are major technical problems that could prevent Safari from not responding or failing to load the webpage.

1. **Wi-Fi Network:** First and foremost ensure that there is an effective network in the Wi-Fi connection on your iPhone.
   - ✓ **Problem 1:** If your Wi-Fi network is perfectly connected and there is no visible network indication on your iPhone.
   - ✓ **Solution 1:** Relocate yourself to a place where you can see the Wi-Fi network because the stronger the Wi-Fi network, the faster Safari's response to loading the webpage.

How to Reactivate Wi-Fi Network in Setting

On Homescreen: Tap on the **Settings Icon**

On Settings: Select **Wi-Fi**

On Wi-Fi: Turn Off the **Wi-Fi** Activator 40secs and put it On again. Go back to Settings and select **Mobile Data.**

Mobile Data: Turn Off the **Mobile Data** Activator for a 40secs and turn it On again. Go back to Settings and select **General**

General: Select **Reset**

Reset

> ➢ Select **Reset Network Settings**
> ➢ Tap on the **Enter Password** that will show below.

Enter Password: Type in the **Password** and confirm the **Safari.**

Second Possible Problem

> ✓ **Problem 2:** If you are having a strong Wi-Fi network and Safari is not responding or loading a webpage.
> ✓ **Solution 2:** Crosscheck the Safari settings as some had been stated above and while the rest will be discussed below under **Settings.**

2. **Settings Crosschecking:** Initially go through all the Safari Settings above. Move a little further by tapping on **Advanced** to confirm the various activations Safari Settings.

On Homescreen: Tap on **Settings Icon**

Settings: Scroll down to select **Safari**

Safari: Start verifying the activated buttons one by one till you get to **Advanced.** Tap on the **Advanced.**

> **Advanced:** Tap on each activation button to turn it Off and turn it On again. If you have not activated the below features on your iPhone before ensure that they are all activated because they are very important.
> ✓ **Advanced:** Initially turn Off the feature one by one to confirm the Safari response, if it is working fine. But, if it is not yet responding turn On the feature and repeat the same action on the next feature till you get the one that is responsible for the Safari abnormality.

- Re-turn On the **JavaScript** activation button.
- Select **Experimental Features.**

✓ **Experimental WebKit Features**
  - Turn Off & Turn On **Blank anchor target implies...** activation button.
  - Turn Off & Turn On **Fetch API Request KeepAlive ...** activation button.
  - Turn Off & Turn On **Quick to prevent delayed initial pain...** activation button.
  - Turn Off & Turn On **Intersection Observer...** activation button.
  - Turn Off & Turn On **Media Capabilities Extensions** activation button.
  - Turn Off & Turn On **Pointer Events** activation button.
  - Re-put On **Swap Processes on Cross-Site...** activation button.
  - Turn Off & Turn On **Synthetic Editing Commands** activation button.
  - Turn Off & Turn On **Block top-level redirects by third...** activation button.
  - Turn Off & Turn On **Visual Viewport API** activation button.
  - Turn Off & Turn On **WebRTC H264 Simulcast** activation button.
  - Turn Off & Turn On **WebRTC mDNS ICE Candidates** activation button.
  - Turn Off & Turn On **WebRTC Unified Plan** activation button.
  - Turn Off & Turn On the **WebRTC VP8** activation button.
  - Turn Off & Turn On **Disable Web SQL** activation button.

CHAPTER SIX

All You Can Do on Camera and Photo Apps on Your iPhone XR

You can use the Camera app to record videos and take pictures of every image around you. The Camera is designed to take live pictures and modify compressed Panorama images. All the captured photographs are automatically saved in Photo Library.

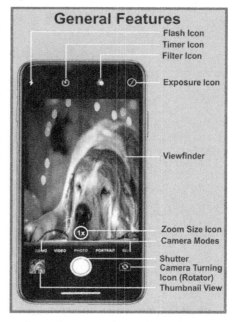

In the Camera interface, you will see options that can be used to take different pictures and what you can do to add more attraction to the pictures.

The Camera can be used to take photographs of anything including flowering plants, animals, humans, and nonliving things at the back and front of your iPhone by tapping on the Camera rotating icon which "I called Camera Rotator" that can change the *rear (back) facing Camera* to *front-facing Camera* to take Selfie.

The different modes in your Camera include; Time-Lapse, Slo-Mo, Video, Photo Mode, Portrait, and Pano (Panorama).

To add more lovely effects to your picture, you can use Filter, Night Mode, Live Photo, and Burst.

106

What You Can See On the Camera Screen

1. Flash Icon: It is at the top left angle of the screen.
2. Night Mode Icon: It is located on the immediate site of the Flash.
3. Live Photo Icon: It is located at the right to the angle of the screen.
4. Edit Toolbar Menu Icon: It is located at the top center of the screen.
5. View Frame: It is located at the center of the screen where the image will appear.
6. Zoom Range: It is at the base of the View Frame to adjust the size of your image.
7. Camera Modes in Row: It is at the top of the Shutter frame.
8. Thumbnail: It is at the left bottom of the screen to show a newly snapped image.
9. Shutter Button: It is at the bottom center of the screen to snap image(s).
10. Camera Rotator Icon: It is at the bottom right of the screen.

There are various ways you can open a Camera on your iPhone.

On Lock-Screen

> Slide your iPhone screen from the right side to the left at the Lock-screen.
> Tap on the **Camera icon** at the bottom right of the iPhone screen.

On Homescreen

> Tap on the **Camera Icon**
> Position the Camera to focus the image at the center of the Viewfinder Screen.
> Tap on the Shutter or Up or Down Volume Button on the left side of your iPhone.

107

To Preserve Your Photograph

On Homescreen: Tap on **Setting Icon**

On Settings: Select **Camera**

On Camera: Select **Preserve Settings**

On Preserve Settings: Turn On the **Live Photo, Camera Mode,** and **Creative Control** Activators.

How to Make Clear & Quality Pictures in a Dark Environment

To prevent night defects on your photograph you have to make use of **Flash** Feature to completely remove shadow or reflection of darkness on your picture exposure quality.

You benefit from another advanced darkness preventing mode called **Night Mode** on your iPhone XR if you can upgrade the iOS 12 to iOS 13.

Look at the top left side corner of the Camera interface you will see the Flash icon; tap on the Flash icon to see select "ON".

When you re-touch the Flash icon, it will be INACTIVE that is, it will go off.

How to Take Quality Photos

You can take photos in a portrait by positioning your iPhone in the normal vertical position ▯ or landscape ▬ by making the iPhone to be positioned in a horizontal position (i.e. the breadth side is longer than the height side of the photo).

On Homescreen: Tap on **Camera Icon**

On Camera

> ➢ Tap on the **PHOTO** App
> ➢ Position the Camera either in Portrait or in Landscape.
> ➢ Let the image be at the center of the Camera Viewfinder.

- ➤ Tap on the **Shutter** or click any of the Volume buttons at the side of your iPhone.
- ➤ You will see the photo in the **Thumbnail** at the bottom left below.
- ➤ Tap on the **Thumbnail** to review the Photo.
- ➤ You may also go to the Photo app to select your snapped picture.
- ➤ **To Delete:** Tap on Photo App and tap on all the pictures you want to delete and tap on **Trash/Waste Bin** at the bottom right of the screen.

Portrait Photo

It is amazing lighting inventions of Photo modification that can make your Photo come out in various professional light exposure to enhance the quality of the image and background.

The lighting effects are *Natural, Studio, Contour, Stage, Stage Light Mono, and High-Key Light Mono* respectively.

On Camera Interface

- ➤ Under the Viewfinder border swipe from **PHOTO** to **PORTRAIT** by swiping from right to left side of the screen.
- ➤ Position your iPhone in Portrait; the various lights will show above the lower region of the Viewfinder in a straight direction but when you place your finger under any of the Lights, the light arrangement will change to arc shape.
- ➤ Tap the ball one by one to see its light effect on the image. Scroll toward the left to see the rest of the light.
- ➤ Let your image be either automatic focus (rectangular) at the center of the Viewfinder or tap any location on the screen to make your focus point.
- ➤ Tap on Shutter to snap the image. You can also do the same for yourself.

Pano Mode (Panorama)

On Homescreen: Tap on **Camera Icon**

On Camera Interface

➢ Under the Viewfinder border swipe from **PORTRAIT** to **PANO** by swiping from right to left side of the screen
➢ First, let the Camera capture the left end of the image.
➢ Tap on Shutter to start capture
➢ Slowly move the Camera straight in an arc ⌒ direction to capture the other end of the image. Use the straight-line arrow on your iPhone.
➢ Tap on the same Shutter to stop the shot.
➢ The Image will be spherically wide in size and look beautiful.
➢ You cannot use it to make Selfies.

Live Photo

On Homescreen: Tap on **Camera Icon**

➢ Look at the lower base of the View Frame scroll from either left to right or right to left to select **Photo**
➢ Tap on the **Live** icon at the top right side of the Camera interface, the icon will change to yellow and you will see LIVE at the top center of the page.
➢ Let the Camera capture image correctly within a rectangle that is automatically showing at the center of the view fame.
➢ Tap on Shutter to take a shot of the image.
➢ The Image will be saved in the Photo library as a Live Photo.

Zoom Capture

The Zoom sizes are shown at the lower base of the View Frame. If the image you want to capture is very small in the **Camera View** you can tap on either time 1 or times 2 to enlarge the image on your screen.

Finger Method

You can place your thumb and a finger on the screen and move them away from each other to enlarge the image or pitch the screen to reduce the image. When you move the two fingers together it will reduce the image size.

Add Effect on a Saved or Recently Snapped Photo in the Library

Camera Interface:

> Look at the bottom left of the Camera you will see a small rectangle showing the recently snapped image, it is called **Thumbnail**.
> Tap on the **Thumbnail** to view the recent image on the Viewfinder. Swipe from right to left to see more pictures you have shot before.
> Tap the image you want to edit.
> Tap the **Filter Icon** ⬤ to change to ⬤ at the top center of the screen. Under the viewfinder, you will see the chosen image appears in a different color of thumbnails.
> Be tapping on the small square photos one by one to choose the best Photo.
> Tap on **Done** to save the selected image at the bottom right of the screen.

Use Burst Shot for Multiple Photo Shots at a Goal

This will enable you to take a continuous photo shot that you can later select the nice pictures among the total shots.

On Camera Interface:

> Let your iPhone Camera be positioned at the image.
> Use your finger to move the **Shutter** to the right without you lifting your finger till you complete all the number of **Burst Shots** you wanted to take within a few seconds.
> The Camera will continue to snap the image.
> Remove your finger from the Shutter, for it to return to the center and stop the continuous shots.

How to Improve the Efficiency of Video & Slo-Mo Recording

The efficiency of Video mode is solely depending on the number of frames per second. The same thing is also applicable to the quality Slo-Mo recording.

However, the high dynamic (HD) revolution for Video recording is higher than the high dynamic for Slo-Mo.

Therefore, through Camera settings, you can wisely improve the quality and efficiency of the Video and Slo-Mo recording.

Video could record at the HD 4K at 60fps (frame per second) and the Slo-Mo could record at the 1080p HD at 240fps when you have more storage capacity on your iPhone.

You can buy sufficient storage from the iCloud store to enhance the high efficiency of the video and slo-mo recording on your iPhone.

Now, to have the best of the normal Video and Slo-Mo Video production on your iPhone with the highest quality resolution you have to initially do the following regulation in the Camera Settings before you start the recording.

On Homescreen: Tap on **Settings Icon**

On Settings: Select **Camera**

On Camera: Tap on **Record SLO-MO**

> **Record SLO-MO:** Select **1080p HD** at **240fps** (frame per second), return to **Camera** settings by tapping on **Back Icon** at the top left of the screen

Camera: Tap on **Record Video**

> **Record Video**

> ➤ Select **4k at 60fps**.
> ➤ Hit on **Back Icon** to return to **Camera** settings.

Camera: Tap on **Format**

Format: Tap on **High Efficiency**

➢ Return to the **Homescreen.**

Homescreen: Tap on **Camera App Icon**

Camera Interface

➢ Select **Video** from the Camera Modes below View margin.
➢ Tap on the Red Recording Button to **Start** the recording.
➢ tap on the button again to Stop the **Video Recording.**

Slo-Mo (Slow Motion)

You can apply motion with a timer to beautify modeling, sports activities, production stages, advertisement, growth... and many others.

Camera Interface: Below the View-frame scroll the Camera mode and tap on **Slo-Mo**.

➢ Position your iPhone either in Portrait or Landscape the best way you want it.
➢ Tap on the Red Recording Button at the bottom center to start either **Selfie Slo-Mo** or Scene/Event/Action taking place at the front of your Camera.
➢ Tap on the Red Recording Button again to Stop the **Slo-Mo Recording.**
➢ **To Play Your Recorded Slo-Mo:** Go to Homescreen and tap on **Photo App.**

Tap on the Slo-Mo and it will play. You can share with your friends in iMessage, Social Media by tapping **Share Icon** at the bottom of the screen.

CHAPTER SEVEN

How to Accurately Track Your Health on Your iPhone XR

You could comfortably study your health wellness by navigating and recording all your health histories in the Health App. The health app will help you generate data for all the total activities you have performed daily, weekly, monthly, and yearly.

Automatically, Health App tracks your daily distance running exercise, gradual physical steps, walk, sleep, mental stability, fertility status, diets, weight balance... and several others. If you are also having Apple Watch it could perform the same function of tracking your daily activities and generate relative data to compare with the previous days.

More data (information) could be gotten from all your relevant Apps such as Calendar, Reminder, Workout, Activity ... and other apps that are helping you in organizing your daily activities and execution of health projects or daily, weekly, monthly, or yearly budgets.

In some cases like a heart condition, menstrual cycle... and others, it is very important that you make use of Apple Watch with your iPhone XR running with iOS 13 to 14, to benefit more perfect health prediction, advanced and efficient Health App.

However, I will discuss some of the vital activities you could track with the use of your iPhone XR running with iOS 12 but when it comes to the activities that could be accurately achieved in iOS 13, I will recommend the upgrade of the default iOS 12 of your iPhone XR to iOS 13 – 14 to efficiently benefit all the features on your iPhone. An example of the activities is *Cycle Tracking.*

What To Do First

You will need to register your Medical Details in these three profile sections:

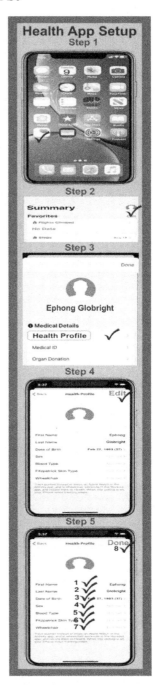

1. **Health Profile:** It contains your Name, Contact, Date of Birth, Sex, Blood Type, Fitzpatrick Skin Type, and Wheelchair.
2. **Medical ID:** It shows the same Emergency information on your iPhone or Apple watch which also contains activation of Emergency when your iPhone is Locked, Date of Birth (DOB), Medical Conditions, Medical Notes, Allergies & Reactions, Medication, Blood Type, Organ Donor, Weight, Height, and Emergency Contacts.
3. **Organ Donation:** This will enable you to register for an Organ donor through the **sign-up with Donate Life.** It comprises the following data of yours; Names, DOB, Last 4 Social Security Number (SSN), Email, Address, ZIP, and Sex.

How You Can Set Up Your Health Profile

On Homescreen: Tap on the **Health App** icon.

On Health: Tap on the **Summary Tab**.

On Summary: Tap on your **Profile Picture** at the top right side of the page.

On **Your Name Page**: Tap on the **Health Profile**

Health Profile:

> ➤ Tap on the **Edit** at the top right corner of the page.
> ➤ Provide your Age, Weight, and Height
> ➤ Tap on **Done** at the top right angle of the page.

How You Can Set Up Medical ID

On **Homescreen**: Tap on the **Health App** icon.

On **Today Page**: Tap on the **Medical ID icon** at the bottom right of the screen ✱

On **Medical ID**: Tap on the **Create Medical ID** bar.

✱ Medical ID

> ➤ Tap on the "**Show When Locked**" activation slider to enable you to access Emergency when your iPhone is locked.
> ➤ Tap on the **Add Photo** to upload your photo on the page
> ➤ Tap on the **Add Date of Birth:** You will see the suggested date at the bottom of the screen. Scroll up until you get the Month/Day/Year of your date

116

of birth and tap on it to select.

➢ Tap on the **Medical Condition** to type your health discomfort (e.g. Herpes, Stomach ache, Arthritis, etc.).

➢ Tap on the **Medical Notes** to write medical history.

➢ Tap on the **Allergies & Reactions** to write the signs and symptoms in the text field. If you do not have any reaction you may write "Nil/None".

➢ Tap on the **Medication** to write the doctor's prescription on the text field. If you do not have, you may type "Nil/None"

➢ Tap on the **Add Blood Type** to select.

➢ Tap on the **Organ Donor** to select "No, Yes or Not Yet"

➢ Tap on the **Weight** to select your body weight.

➢ Tap on the **Height** to select your height.

➢ Tap on the **Add Emergency Contact** to select your trusted loved ones' contact from your iPhone contact list.

➢ Tap on **Done** at the top right corner of the screen.

How To Setup Emergency Through Health App

➢ Press the **Power** Button to sleep and re-press the button to wake the iPhone.

➢ Use your Face ID to unlock the iPhone.

➢ Swipe up from the bottom center of the screen to see the lock screen with the **Emergency** at the bottom left of the screen.

➢ Tap on the **Emergency**

➢ **Emergency Call:** If you must access Medical ID, then tap the **Medical ID** at the bottom left of the screen. All the information you have provided during the setup will appear.

➢ At the bottom of the Medical ID page, you will see the **Continue bar**. Tap on the **Continue** bar to complete the registration.

➢ Tap on **Complete Registration with Donate later** bar.

➢ **Thank You:** Tap on the **Done** bar.

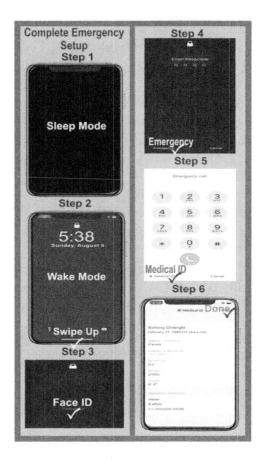

How to Setup Your Health Data

If you have previously upgraded your iPhone XR from iOS 12 to 13 version, the below steps will be seen on your upgraded iPhone XR.

But, if your iPhone XR is running iOS 12, the below steps will be slightly advanced than the steps of the Health app on your iPhone.

On Homescreen: Tap on the **Health App** icon.

On Dashboard: You will see your **Dashboard**. There are period titles which are **Day | Week | Month | Year.** You can select any of the periods that you will be tracking your health data. To start with, select **Day** by tapping on it.

118

Tap on the **Health Data** at the bottom second left of the screen to add different health categories such as **Body Weight, Active Calories, Heart Record, Heart, Reproductive Health, Body Temperature ...** and more others.

For Instance:

> ➢ Tap on the **Active Calories**
> ➢ Active Calories: Tap on **Add Data Point.**
> ➢ Add Data:
>> ✓ Type Your daily preferred Calories figure like 250
>> ✓ Tap on **Add** at the top right corner of the screen.

You will see that the number of Calories has been increased from the recommended calories per day. But if you are not having calories on the displayed table, you could go ahead and add your daily calories.

Your iPhone will strictly use your daily recommended calories to track your daily calories used throughout your daily activities.

For the tracking to show on your Dashboard, then you have to activate the "**Show on Dashboard**" switch slider.

Now as you are moving or walking around, the number of your steps, distance cover in Kilometer (Km), and Calories spent (kcal) will be tracked.

To Add More of Your Health History

On Homescreen: Tap on the **Health App** icon.

On Health Data

> ➢ Tap on the **Browse** tab

- ➢ Tap on a **Category** like Activity.
- ➢ Select **Subcategory** like Steps
- ➢ Tap on the **Add Data** at the top right corner of the screen.
- ➢ Type the **Date, Time,** and **Data** for the Activity.
- ➢ Tap on **Add** at the top right angle of the screen.

How to Check Your Health Data

On Homescreen: Tap on the **Health App** icon.

On Health Data: tap on the **Category** like **Body Measurement**

On Body Measurement: Select your **Subcategory** like **Body Mass Index**.

Body Mass Index

- ➢ Turn "On" the **Add to Favorite** activator.
- ➢ Hit on the "**Show All Data**" to see all the data of the tracked activity.
- ➢ After you have confirmed what you want to know then you can back the page at the top left corner of the page.

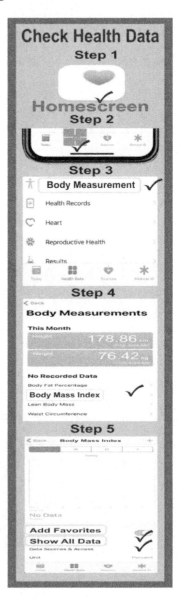

How to Track All Your Favorite Categories within Your iPhone XR

On Homescreen: Tap on the **Health App** icon

Today Summary: Tap on the **Summary Tab**

Summary: Tap on the **Edit** at the top right corner of the screen page.

Edit Favorite

- ➤ Tap on each desirable **Star** to add more **Categories**★
- ➤ As soon as you have completely selected all your preferred **Favorite Categories**, then tap on **Done** at the top right side of the screen.
  Note: When you tap on each star, it will change from framed star ☆ to blue filled star★

How to Set Up Organ Donation

On Homescreen: Tap on the **Health App** icon.

On Health: Tap on the **Summary Tab**.

On Summary: Tap on your **Profile Picture** at the top right side of the page.

Your Name Page: Select **Organ Donor**

Organ Donor: Tap on the **Sign Up with Donate Life** bar to sign up.

Registration

- ➤ All your profile details will display, what you only need to do is to enter the last four-digit number of your **Social Security Number** (SSN).
- ➤ Tap on the **Continue** button below to complete your registration.

➢ Tap on the "**Complete Registration with Donate Life**" at the bottom center of the screen.

Thank You: Tap on the **Done** button below.

Your complete registration with Donate Life will show up under your Medical ID profile as **Organ Donor-Donate Life.**

How You Can Solve Health Tracking Steps Failure on Your iPhone XR

For your health tracking steps to be functionally perfect, you need to connect your Apple Watch with your iPhone.

If you are having a challenge of not seeing your steps being tracked by Health App on your iPhone XR, then take the following steps:

On Homescreen: Tap on the **Health App** icon.

On Health: Tap on the **Summary Tab**.

On Summary: Tap on your **Profile Picture** at the top right side of the page.

On Your Name Page: Under **Privacy** tap on the **Devices**

On Devices: Select your **Apple Watch**

Your Watch Privacy: tap on **Privacy Settings** and activate **Fitness Tracking** by switching On the Activator.

How to Set Up Family Sharing

On Homescreen: Tap on the **Settings App** icon

On Settings: Go to your **Profile Name** at the top

On Apple ID: Select "**Set Up Family Sharing**".

On Family Sharing: Tap on the "**Get Started**" button

Get Started: Select **Location Sharing** or any other feature you want to share. There might be a slightly different method of setup in various other features of family sharing available.

Share Your Location with Your Family: Tap on the **"are Your Location"** button at the bottom center of the screen. If you are not ready to share your location you can select the "**Not Now**" option below.

Invite Your Family: Tap on the "**Invite Family Members**" bar at the bottom center.

How to Track Your Menstrual Cycle with Your iPhone XR

The use of Health apps to track women's menstrual cycle can only be studied and determined when you upgrade the default iOS 12 version on your iPhone to iOS 13; and watchOS 6 if you are using a watch.

However, you must use Apple Watch with your iPhone XR running with iOS 13 to benefit more from the innovativeness and efficiency loaded in the Health App.

How You Can Set Up Every Month Menstrual Cycle on Your iPhone XR

On Homescreen: Tap on the **Health App** icon.

On Search: Tap on the **Browse** tab at the bottom right of the screen. ▧▧.

On Browse:

> ➤ Select **Cycle Tracking** among the **Health Categories**
> ➤ Tap on the "**Get Started**" button.

On Cycle Tracking: Tap on **Options**

On Options

> ➤ You will scroll down to select **Period Length** and swipe up to select your period duration e.g. 2 days, 3 days, 4 days, 5days, etc. The period length is the number of days you experience menstrual flow. For example, If you see your menstrual flow from Aug 2 to 5 is equal to 4days.

> Select **Cycle Length** and swipe up to select the appropriate days before the next menstrual cycle e.g. 25 days or 26 days etc.

Hint: If you are having some pre or post symptoms that come with your cycle you may activate all the relevant suggested contents above **Your Cycle Log.** Some of them are:

1. Spotting
2. Basal Body Temperature
3. Cervical Mucus Quality
4. Ovulation Test Result
5. Sexual Activity
6. Symptoms… and others.

How to See Your Cycle Timeline

On Homescreen: Tap on the **Health App** icon.

On Search: Tap on the **Browse** tab at the bottom right of the screen.

Browse: Select **Cycle Tracking** among the **Health Categories**

The Timeline will appear as:

1. **Solid Circles**: Number of days you recorded for your menstrual period.
2. **Purple Dots**: The number of days you recorded for experiencing symptoms
3. **Light Red Circle:** This is your next menstrual period Prediction.
   ✓ **For You to Hide or Display Predicted Period Days:** Select **Option** and activate the **Period Prediction** switch.

4. **Light Blue Days:** These predict your possible Fertility Window. You should not use it to guide yourself for birth control.
   ✓ **For You to Hide or Display Infertility Window:** Select **Option** and activate the **Fertility Prediction** switch.

How You Can Know Your Possible Next Menstrual Cycle

On Homescreen: Tap on the **Health App** icon.

On Search: Tap on the **Browse** tab at the bottom right of the screen.

On Browse: Select **Cycle Tracking** among the **Health Categories**

Cycle Tracking

➢ Scroll down to select **Prediction** under **Cycle Log.** This will enable you to know your next menstrual cycle.
   ✓ **If you are unable to see the evaluation:** Select **Show All** before the prediction option.
➢ Scroll down to select **Statistics.** This will enable you to see all your previous menstrual periods and predictive cycle length.

On Apple Watch: For You to Determine Date
➢ Launch the "**Cycle Track App**".
➢ Scroll down to select "**Period Prediction/Last Menstrual Period**".

How You Can Track All Your Cycle Symptoms in Health App

On Homescreen: Tap on the **Health App** icon.

127

On Search: Tap on the **Browse** tab at the bottom right of the screen. ▪▪

Browse: Select **Cycle Tracking** among the **Health Categories**

Cycle Tracking: Tap on **Options** at front of **Cycle Log**

Options: Activate the **Symptoms** activator ⬭ to access all the possible symptoms before/during/after the menstrual cycle. All the symptoms are listed below:

- ✓ Abdominal Cramp
- ✓ Acne
- ✓ Appetite
- ✓ Bloating
- ✓ Breast Tenderness
- ✓ Constipation
- ✓ Diarrhea
- ✓ Headache
- ✓ Hot Flashes
- ✓ Lower Back Pain
- ✓ Mood Changes
- ✓ Nausea
- ✓ Ovulation Pain
- ✓ Tiredness
- ✓ Sleep Changes

You can tap on any of the symptoms you are experiencing before or during or after the menstrual cycle to log (record) your symptoms with Cycle Tracking.

How You Can Record Menstrual Cycle Symptoms on Your Apple Watch.

On Apple Watch:

➢ To launch Apple tray by pressing **Digital Crown**

128

➤ Select the **Cycle Tracking** App icon
➤ Tap on **Symptoms**
➤ Scroll through the various available symptoms and tap on various symptoms lists you regularly experience before, during, or after the menstrual cycle.
➤ Tap on **Done**

How You Can Set Up Prediction for Period, fertility, and Notification, through Cycle Tracking

How You Can Track All Your Cycle Symptoms in Health App

On Homescreen: Tap on the **Health App** icon.

On Search: Tap on the **Browse** tab at the bottom right of the screen.

Browse: Select **Cycle Tracking** among the **Health Categories**

Cycle Tracking: Tap on **Options**

Options: Tap on the activator of the below features to turn them "On".

➤ Activate **Period Prediction**.
➤ Activate the **Period Notification.**
➤ Activate the **Fertility Predictions**
➤ Activate **Fertility Notifications.**

How You Can Record A Period Flow Level Through Cycle Tracking on Your Apple Watch

On Apple Watch

- ➢ To launch the Apple tray, press **Digital Crown**

- ➢ Select the **Cycle Tracking** App icon
- ➢ In the everyday tracker above the data, & Summary, tap on the **Day.**
- ➢ Below Menstrual Unit, tap on **Period** to record your menstrual flow. Select your period flow level by tapping on any of these options below:
  - ✓ Light
  - ✓ Medium
  - ✓ Heavy
- ➢ Tap on **Done.**

How You Can Further Record Your Sexual Activity In Cycle Tracking

You can use this to track the last time or the period you had sex with your spouse.

On Option:

- ➢ Tap on **Sexual Activity**
- ➢ On the same page, tap on **Sexual Activity** and select **Had Sex**.
- ➢ Select **Not Used** or **Used** to remind you of your sexual protection.

How You Can Record Your Sexual Activity in Cycle Tracking on Your Apple Watch

On Apple Watch

- ➢ To launch the Apple tray, press **Digital Crown**

- ➢ Select the **Cycle Tracking** App icon

130

- ➤ Tap on the **Sexual Activity**
- ➤ If you had sexual intercourse, then tap on **Had Sex**
- ➤ For protection confirmation, select **Not Used** or **Used.**

How You Can Remove All Cycle Tracking in Health App On Your iPhone.

On Homescreen: Tap on the **Health App** icon.

On Search: Tap on the **Browse** tab at the bottom right of the screen.

Browse: Select **Cycle Tracking** among the **Health Categories**

Cycle Tracking: Scroll down to select "**View Cycle Tracking Items**".

View Cycle Tracking Items: Tap on every **Category Log** you wanted to remove.

- ➤ Scroll down to the bottom region to tap on the "**Show All Data**".
- ➤ At the top right corner of the screen, tap on **Edit.**
- ➤ Tap on the **Remove icon** beside the data you wanted to remove.
- ➤ Tap on **Delete.**
- ➤ Tap on **Done** at the top right angle of the screen.

How to Locate the Data Source from Several Sources

Health App always gathers many data (information) from different sources like Apple Watch, iPhone, and iPod. If you are using several Apple devices that are connected with iPhone XR, it very important as a user to specifically know which of the Apple device is responsible for the data making.

You can set your iPhone to be the major source that Health App should be used for data generation, instead of using all available Bluetooth devices. This method is called the **Prioritization of Device.**

On Homescreen: Tap on the **Health App** to launch the page.

On Summary: Tap on the **Browse** icon tab.

On Browse: Tap on a **Category** such as **Activity**.

On Activity: Select the **Subcategory** such as Steps or Walk & Running or any other one.

Hint: But if you are unable to see the subcategory you are looking for, then you can scroll up to use the *Searching field tool* at the top of the page. Tap the field and enter the **Subcategory** and it will appear.

Steps: Swipe up to select **Data Sources & Access**

Hint: You will see all the Sources that are responsible for creating the Steps' Data will be enlisted.

How to Access All The General Sources For The Health App

On Homescreen: Tap on the **Health App** to launch the page.

On Summary: Tap on **Profile Picture** at the top right of the page.

On Your Profile Name Page: Scroll down the page to Privacy and tap on **Apps or Devices.**

You will see all the Sources that enable Health App to generate those Data.

How You Can Assign Sources for Data

This will enable you to arrange sources for generating a particular subcategory's data in the Health App.

On Homescreen: Tap on the **Health App** to launch the page.

On Summary: Tap on the **Browse** icon tab.

On Browse: Tap on a **Category** such as **Activity.**

Activity: Select the **Subcategory**

Subcategory: You will go down the page and select **Data Source & Access.**

Data Source & Access: tap on **Edit**

> Touch and Hold down **Change Order** Button at the front of the Data Source.
> You can either **Drag Up** or **Down** the **Data Source** on the lists.

If you do not want a Data Source to generate Data for the Subcategory: Deactivate the **Activation Switch**

CHAPTER EIGHT

How to Perform the Complete Security IDs on Your iPhone XR

How to Achieve a Protective Apple ID

Apple ID will protect your vital documents, Apple Pay Credit Card; it will enable you to buy more applications on your iPhone, create more lively activities, activation, or settings of different apps... and many others.

You need to have one Apple ID to link all your Apple devices like Apple iPhones, iPods, Macbook, iMac, Mac, and Watch together. That is if you are privileged to have more than one iPhones or different types of Apple device.

How To Create Your Apple ID Process

1. Homescreen Approach the Settings Icon by tapping on it.
2. Settings: Look at the side of Profile Picture at the top and tap on **Sign In to Your iPhone.**
3. Apple ID
   - ➢ In the Email text field, type your active **Email Address**.
   - ➢ Look at the top right corner of the screen to tap on **Next.**
   - ➢ Select **"Don't Have An Apple ID"**
   - ➢ An informative Dialog box will come up, tap on the option of **"Create Apple ID".**
4. Date of Birth
   - ➢ Type in your **Date of Birth** in the provided text field.
   - ➢ At the top corner of the screen, tap on the **Next.**
5. Name: Enter your **Name and Last Name** into the text field and tap on **Next.**
6. Email

- ➢ Make sure you enter the **Email** without a typographical mistake or choose "**Get Free iCloud Email Address**" and tap on the **Next** option.
- ➢ If you choose "**Free iCloud Email**" tap on the **Next** and **Continue.**

Password

- ➢ You will be allowed two times to type your **Password.** Type the same password in the first password text field into the second verify password text field. If incorrect, it won't continue.
- ➢ Make your password be eight digits, having a combination of a number, uppercase, and lowercase alphabetical letters.
- ➢ Tap on the **Next** at the top to continue.

7. Phone Number
- ➢ Carefully choose your Country
- ➢ Type your **Phone Number** for your identity verification.

8. Verification Method: Select any of the below options:
- ➢ **Text Message**
- ➢ **Phone Call**
- ➢ Confirm your option with **Checkmark** and tap on **Next**

9. Security Questions
- ➢ Give an unforgettable answer to the security question you are asked. You can write the question and the answer into

135

your confidential organizer/planner to subsequently guide you to provide the exact answer whenever you are asked to answer the question during an essential activity on your iPhone.

10. **Verification Code**
➢ Type the **Text 6-Digits Code** sent to you through your iPhone Message into the **Verification designated space** for the **Code.**

11. **Terms and Conditions**
➢ Read through the terms and conditions, digest, and get used to them or familiarize yourself with them because it is very important. Tap on **Agree** at the bottom right. If you **Disagree,** it implies that you are not in support of Apple's Terms and Conditions guiding the Apple ID ownership, as a result, the Apple ID process will be discontinued and terminated.

12. **Enter iPhone Passcode:** Type your iPhone **Passcode** (4 or 6 digits). If you do not have a passcode, go to the **Add Passcode** page on the section to learn how to create your iPhone Passcode.

13. **iCloud**
➢ For iCloud to get documents

136

from Contact, Reminder, Notes, Calendar, and Safari on your iPhone. Tap on the **Merge** option.

➢ You may consider the other option of **Don't Merge** if you are having any other opinion on their synchronization.

14. Find My iPhone Dialog Box

➢ On the Dialog box accept by tapping on **OK.**

Hint: You will see your Full Name appear where you saw Sign in to Your iPhone. Anytime you want to sign in to your iPhone, tap on your name and continue.

Now, you have created an Apple ID for yourself. Please you need to keep email & password details carefully to prevent false operators or fraudsters from using your iPhone for illegal activities.

How To Change Your Apple ID Process

On Homescreen: Launch the Settings Icon by tapping on it.

On Settings: Look at the Profile Name beside Profile Picture at the top tap on **Name.**

Password & Security

➢ Tap on the **Change Password**
➢ Type in your valid **Password.**
➢ Type in your **New Password**
➢ Type in your **New Password** again for confirmation
➢ Tap on **Change Password**

How To Sign In Apple ID On Your iPhone Process

On Homescreen: Launch the **Settings Icon** by tapping on it.

On Settings: Look at the Profile Name beside Profile Picture at the top tap on **Sign In to Your iPhone.**

Apple ID

➢ In the Email text field, type your active **Email Address**.

137

➢ Look at the top right corner of the screen to tap on **Next.**
In the **Password text field** type in complex and easy to remember **Password.** Better still, write it into your confidential organizer.

➢ Look at the top right angle of the screen to tap on **Next.**

➢ In the last part of the page, you will see Sign Out and tap on it to leave the page.

Now, you have added your Apple ID to your iPhone.

How To Recover Your Forgot Apple ID Process

On Homescreen: Approach the **Settings Icon** by tapping on it.

On Settings: Look at the Profile Name beside the Profile Picture at the top tap on **Sign In to Your iPhone.**

Apple ID:

➢ First and foremost, type your correct Email add into the email text field.

➢ Look below you will see a 2-in-1 question state thus, **Don't have an Apple ID or Forgot it?**

➢ Tap on **Forgot it.**

➢ **On Informative Box** tap on **Forgot Apple ID.**

➢ Firstly, you will type in a new **Password,** and secondly, type the same password for the system to verify the correctness.

➢ Go to the top right angle of the screen to tap on **Next.**

You can verify it by tapping on Sign In, Type your submitted email, tap next, type your new approved Password, and tap next.

How You Can Correctly Do Your Face ID

Face ID is another defensive mechanism/tool you can use to prevent fake users from using your iPhone. The use of Face ID on your iPhone will strongly enhance your iPhone security. It can be used to Unlock your iPhone.

You can use Face ID to buy things from iTunes Store, Apple Store, Apple Book with the use of your Apple pay.

Face ID in these modern developed iPhones XR has replaced Touch ID in the lower iPhones, as a result, you will see Face ID & Passcode together under Settings on your new iPhone not Touch ID & Passcode.

But, it is less effective among identical twins that are physically looking alike. It will be difficult for your iPhone Face ID infrared sensor to identify or differentiate the facially identical people.

How You Can Create Face ID Through Settings Process

On Homescreen: Approach the **Settings Icon** by tapping on it.

On Settings: Search down to tap on **Set Up Face ID.**

Camera

> The Camera should be positioned in a portrait to capture your face. Don't allow any other person to stay behind you when you are taking your face.
> Tap on the "**Get Started**" bar.
> Let your face be boldly covered in the Camera center of the Viewfinder.
> Focus your eyes on the Front-Facing Camera Sensor and let your head be in the middle of the Viewfinder of the Camera.
> As you are turning your head gradually the surrounding lines of the Viewfinder will be changing to green, keep turning your head and let every side of your head be captured by the Camera sensor. You should not stop until the Viewfinder surrounding lines are completely changed to green.
> If the first Face ID scanner is successful, tap on the **Continue** bar and turn your head in either the same or opposite way again, once the second Face ID scanner is complete, tap on the **Done** bar.

Hint: If you are unable to turn your head or stiff neck, tap on **Accessibility.**

How to Create a Strong & Safe Passcode

Most of the time, your iPhone will always ask you to create a personal Passcode to alternate Face ID to unlock your iPhone. In a situation where you are having an identical twin-face, the Face ID may compromise. This means you should have a Passcode that you alone can provide. Therefore, you can use the Passcode to prevent your twin/close relatives from accessing your iPhone without your consent.

In a situation whereby the Face ID failed to identify your face because of the face transformation you applied (i.e. face mask, excessive face makeup, etc.) your iPhone will automatically request for your iPhone's Passcode.

More so, your iPhone will ask for Passcode anytime you perform the below tasks on your iPhone:

> For Installation of iOS
> Restarting or Switching On of Your iPhone.
> To Remove/Delete All The Data on Your iPhone.
> To Change or Access Passcode Settings on Your iPhone.
> To Perform Software Update.

How to Create Passcode via Settings Process

On Homescreen: Tap on the **Settings Icon.**

On Settings: Scroll down the page and select the **Face ID & Passcode** option.

On Face ID & Passcode

> Scroll down the page tap on **Turn Passcode On** option.
> By default, you will see 6 digits passcode which you can change to a 4-digits passcode.

140

- But, if you are comfortable with the 6-digits type, then input complex **Passcode** that will have the mixture of Number, Small Case, and Capital Case of Alphabets.
- For 4-digits Passcode, tap on **Passcode Options** above the Keyboard and tap on the third option.
  - ✓ A Custom Alphanumeric Code
  - ✓ A Custom Numeric Code
  - ✓ **4-Digit Numeric Code**
- Re-type the complex Passcode for confirmation

Hint: You have to make your Passcode to be complex to prevent passcode hackers or guessers from predicting your passcode. Therefore, mix the passcode digits by selecting **Alphanumeric Code** and writing it on your planner for record purposes.

Has your Passcode been exposed to the wrong person?

Are you noticing suspicious operations on your iPhone?

Then, take a protective wise approach by changing the present passcode to a new Passcode.

How To Change Exposed Present Passcode Process

On Homescreen: Tap on **Settings Icon**.

On Settings: Search down the page and select the **Face ID & Passcode** option.

Face ID & Passcode: Search down the page and tap on the **Change Passcode** option.

Change Passcode:

- If you are using a 6 or 4-Digits Password, type the insecure Password.
- The New Passcode will be requested to be re-typed twice.

Once you type the last digit, it will automatically approve and move to the previous page.

Activation of Apps in iCloud Account

The activation of apps in the iCloud account will determine the number of apps data that will be automatically uploaded and stored in iCloud storage for you to access from all your devices. There are lots of suggested apps on your iPhone you can backup and store in the iCloud storage.

This can only be done if you switch on those apps on the iCloud page. Follow the below steps to select the appropriate apps that you want to back up with iCloud.

Therefore, you have to make more storage space available on your iPhone.

Example of the Apps is *Photo, Mail, Contacts, Calendars, Reminders, Notes, Messages, Safari, News, Stocks, Home, Health, Wallet, Game Center, and Siri.*

On Homescreen: Approach the **Settings Icon** by tapping on it.

On Settings: Look at the Profile Name beside Profile Picture at the top and tap on **Sign In to Your iPhone.**

Apple ID: Look at the middle of the page and tap on the **iCloud** option.

iCloud: Tap the app's activation switch to change the switch to green.

Keychain:

> ➤ Tap on **Keychain** to turn "On" the **iCloud Keychain** switch.
> ➤ Return to the iCloud page by tapping on the **Back Arrow of iCloud** at the top left angle of the screen.

Hint: In all the devices you are using, it will constantly record the credit card details and password you have accepted.

Find My iPhone

- ➤ Select **Find My iPhone** below the Keychain option under iCloud.
- ➤ tap on **Find My iPhone** switches to activate it.
- ➤ Return to the iCloud page by tapping on the **Back Arrow of iCloud** at the top left angle of the screen.

Hint: This will enable you to locate, lock, activate, or erase your iPhone and other approved equipment if you produce your **Password**.

iCloud Backup

- ➤ Select **iCloud Backup** option
- ➤ Tap on **iCloud Backup** to activate the backup.
- ➤ Return to the iCloud page by tapping on the **Back Arrow of iCloud** at the top left angle of the screen.

iCloud Drive: It will accept all apps to store data and documents in iCloud.

- ➤ Tap on **iCloud Drive** to activate it.
- ➤ Move to the top left of the page to tap on the **Back icon** of Apple ID.
- ➤ Tap on the **Back icon** at the top of Settings and swipe up from the center bottom of the iPhone to go back to the Homescreen.

CHAPTER NINE

How to Find Your Lost iPhone XR

There are some important steps of settings that you have to do on your iPhone which will make the feature of **Find My App** to be active on your iPhone XR.

1. Find Friends and Family Members or
2. Share your location with others
3. Set up **Find My.**

How You Can Activate Find My on Your iPhone

Hint: "**Find My**" is automatically turned on when you Sign In to your new iPhone with your Apple ID, but, there is a need for you to find out if **Find My iPhone, Enable Offline Finding** and **Send Last Location** are activated.

On Homescreen: Tap on the **Settings Icon**

On Settings: Tap on your **Name/Sign In To Your iPhone** beside the profile picture.

On Apple ID: Tap on the" **Find My"**

Find My

> ➤ Tap on the "**Find My iPhone"** to select "**On**" if the

activation feature is **Off.**

Find My iPhone: Turn On the activators of the following if they are Off:

- ✓ **Find My iPhone:** It will always request your Password to locate, erase, or lock your iPhone.
- ✓ **Enable Offline Finding:** Your iPhone will be located even when it is not connected to a cellular or Wi-Fi network.
- ✓ **Send Last Location:** iCloud will automatically send the location of your iPhone to Apple when the battery is drastically low.

➢ Tap on the **My Location** to select **This Device.**
➢ Tap on the **"Share My Location's Activator"** to put on the switch.

What To Do After You Have Lost Your iPhone

There is the possibility of misplacing your iPhone XR in a location that you could not recollect because you had visited more than three places before you could remember that your iPhone is missing or stolen.

Also, you might have kept the iPhone in a compartment that is best known to you only but after a while, you could not remember the specific place you have kept the iPhone.

However, Apple has made a reliable way of locating your iPhone XR with the use of Find My iPhone and iCloud Map Detection or Google Map to specifically describe and show you the location of your iPhone XR wherever it had been kept.

First Finding Solution

On Mac or PC

➢ Use any of the available browsers such as Chrome, Mozilla Firefox, Internet Explorer, Safari, Opera, Lynx, or Konqueror… and many others.
➢ In the Web Add text field type **icloud.com.**

iCloud Homepage:

➤ Sign In with your Apple ID which includes your **Email** and **Password**.

➤ Click on **Find iPhone Icon**  among the icons on the screen.

iCloud Find My iPhone: Location Map will display on the screen.

➤ At the top **bar** center of the screen, click on All Devices.

➤ On the **drop-down & select your iPhone**. (If you are using more than one Apple device that is using the same Apple ID. You will see all the Apple devices on the drop-down).

➤ The Map will zoom out to indicate the iPhone location with a black circle and your iPhone' Name label

➤ At the right corner, you will see 3 options you can use to help your findings
  ✓ Play Sound
  ✓ Lost Mode
  ✓ Erase iPhone

Play Sound: If you are pretty sure that the iPhone is around (home, workshop, or office) then you can click **Play Sound** immediately you will start hearing vibration with sound. The sound will continue until you tap on **Find My iPhone Alert** OK.

Lost Mode: This option is perfect when you discovered that you can no longer recover/find your iPhone again. Then you can click on **Lost Mode.**

- ✓ **Phone Number Dialog Box:** Type your **Phone Number** (that can be called by the finder) and click on **Next** at the top right corner of the dialog box.
- ✓ Click on the Text box, type the message that will be shown on your iPhone XR screen. e.g. **"Please I have lost this iPhone. Kindly Call Me. Thank you"** and click on **Done** at the top right angle of the dialog box.

Automatically the iPhone will be locked. It will only be unlocked if you enter your passcode or through your Face ID.

Erase iPhone: This option is accurate when you realized that the iPhone could not be located, then, click **Erase iPhone** to completely remove all your vital and confidential **data, applications (apps) & documents** from the iPhone quickly.

Second Finding Solution:

This can be used when you are having Google Map App on your iPhone but if you do not have the app you can use the iCloud method above.

On Mac or PC

- ➤ Use any of the available browsers such as Chrome, Mozilla Firefox, Internet Explorer, Safari, Opera, Lynx, or Konqueror.
- ➤ In the Web Add text field type **www.google.com/maps**

Google Maps:

➤ Click on **Menu Icon** at the top left side of the **Search Google Maps Text Field**.

➤ **Menu:** Select **Your Timeline** (Timeline will show various locations you have been with your iPhone on Google maps with an indication of red color).

➤ At the left side of the screen click on **Today** at the front of the **Timeline**.

Immediately, a line will show your different movements on the day in the Google maps to know where your iPhone could be found.

➤ You can zoom in on the map to make the location to be closer and clearer for you to see the location very well.

➤ You can increase the movement line (appear in blue) at the left side of the screen to see more of different places with their specific time in hours, minutes, and seconds that you moved from a particular place to another place till the final place where the iPhone could be found.

Note: You won't see the exact spot where the iPhone could be found on

the Google map but you could only know the environment where you can see the iPhone.

How to Use Another iPhone to Track Your Lost iPhone

The method of tracking your lost iPhone on the computer is virtually the same as the method and processes of locating your lost iPhone on another iPhone.

If you are having two iPhones in your family or your friend has one, you can easily use the available iPhone to quickly discover where your iPhone is kept or the location at which it could be found with either hope of recovery or not.

On Homescreen: Tap on the **Find My** App Icon

On Find My: Tap on the **Devices** icon at the bottom center of your iPhone.

Devices: Tap on your lost **iPhone XR's Name** (e.g. Ephong's iPhone) this means your first name will be used to qualify the lost iPhone.

iPhone XR's Name: Swipe up from the top edge center of the page to select one of the available options below:

1. **Play Sound**: Having 100% assurance of finding it.
2. **Directions**: If it is discovered on the map and you want it to be tracked down,

149

3. **Notifications:** You will be notified when the iPhone is found.
4. **Mark As Lost**: If the recovery chances of your iPhone is| 70 – 80% but the location on the map displayed is extremely far. Then you can tap on **Active.**
5. **Erase This Device**: If the chance of recovering your iPhone is less than 50% which is very narrow, then you can choose the option by tapping it.

Hint: if you eventually select **Erase This Device** because you have initially lost hope of finding it, as a result, you would not be able to track your iPhone again. But, if by slim opportunity you found the iPhone, you will only be able to restore all the erased data and documents on your iPhone through iCloud backup.

How to Share Your Location with Others

You will need to select the people that you want to share your location. This option will enable you to track down your lost iPhone on your friend's iPhone.

On Homescreen: Tap on the "**Find My App Icon**".

Find My: tap on the **People** icon at the

150

bottom left of the screen.

People: Tap on the "**Start Sharing Location**".

Start Sharing Location

> ➤ Type the "**Name of the Person**" you want to share your location into the Text Field and tap on **Send** at the top right angle of the page.
> ➤ An Optional Dialog Box will show up to select "time for the sharing of your location with the person". Select any of the flowing options:
>> ✓ Share for One Hour
>> ✓ Share Until End of Day
>> ✓ Share Indefinitely
> ➤ **Notification:** On a Dialog box you will see "You Shared Your Location with the Person's Contact. Tap on **OK**.

How You Can Setup CarPlay Connection on Your iPhone & Car Stereo

You need to confirm if your car is supporting Apple CarPlay before you start the connection process.

What to Do First
> ➤ Confirm the CarPlay compatibility with your Stereo.
> ➤ Verify if the use of CarPlay is allowed in your area or Country.
> ➤ Start your car, let the screen stereo boot, and show the Homescreen.
> ➤ Perform your iPhone Settings for CarPlay
> ➤ Activate Siri.
> ➤ Update your iOS 11 to iOS 12 or 13 (see "**Update**" in the Chapter)

Activate Siri On Your iPhone

On **Homescreen:** Tap on **Settings**

On Settings: Tap on **Siri & Search**

On Siri & Search: Turn On all the activators.

Different Ways of Connecting CarPlay from Your iPhone XR to Your Car
1. Lightning to USB cable connection.
2. Bluetooth connection.
3. Wireless connection.

Connection Process for USB Car Port
➢ Start your Car and let the Car's Stereo boot to the Homepage.
➢ Insert the small power connector of the USB cable into your iPhone USB power port. Ensure you hear a clear click sound,
➢ Insert the second end of the USB cord into the Stereo USB port.
➢ **Once it is properly connected:** You will see the **Apple CarPlay** icon among the Apps icon on the Car's Homescreen.

Connection Process for Car Using Wireless or Bluetooth
➢ Press and hold down the **Voice-Command** on the Steering Wheel.
➢ **Go to Your iPhone XR**

On Homescreen: Tap on Settings.

On Settings: Scroll down to tap on **General**

On General: Tap on **CarPlay**

On CarPlay

➢ Tap on **Available Car**
➢ Select your Car name.

➢ **Once it is connected:** You will see all the **Apple CarPlay** Icon among the Apps icon on the Car's Homescreen.

On Your Touch Sensitive Stereo
➢ The stereo will restart and show **Caution** information, read and tap on **I Agree**
➢ In a few seconds, the **Apple CarPLay** icon will show.
➢ Tap on the **Apple CarPlay.** All your iPhone Apps (e.g. Call, Music, Messages, Maps, Audiobooks, YouTube, etc.) will display on the Stereo CarPlay Screen. Press the bottom right arrow to see more Apps.

To Add More App to the Default Apps on Your Touch Sensitive Stereo Homescreen

On Homescreen: Tap on Settings.

On Settings: Scroll down to tap on **General**

On General: Tap on **CarPlay**

On CarPlay: Select the Name of your Car (e.g. **SUBARU**)

SUBARU: Tap on **Customize**

Customize: Scroll down the page and select from the Apps under **MORE APP** by tapping on the Add Sign in a green circle in front of the App you want to be added on the Car Stereo Homescreen.

You can also add

153

Google Map to complement Apple Map.

To Remove Apps: Under the **INCLUDE** list of all the default apps on the Car's Homescreen, tap on Minus Sign in a red circle at the front of the App to delete the App from the list. You can restore it by going to the MORE APP and tap on Add sign.

How to Rearrange The Apps On The CarPlay Homescreen

Customize: Tap on the App and drag it either up or down within the Apps. The Apps will show on the CarPlay Homescreen exactly what you arranged them on the **Customized List.**

How to Use Siri to Work for You on CarPlay

Siri is very helpful in giving reliable suggestions through CarPlay to let you know the possible next line of action or sending a message to someone by dictating your message directly.

You can instruct Siri to forward a call to any of your favorite contacts.

However, the type of your car will determine how you can use Siri to do what you want it to do for you.

There are three major ways to use Siri with your CarPlay
1. On the Stereo Sensitive Touchscreen, touch and hold **CarPlay Home** and ask Siri to do it for you.
2. On the Stereo Sensitive Touchscreen, touch and hold **CarPlay Dashboard** and give Siri instructions.
3. On the **Steering Wheel** press and hold the **Voice-Command button** and ask Siri what you want.

To Send Message On CarPlay Through Siri

On Homescreen: Tap on the **Messages App** icon

On **Messages:** Select the **Name of the Person** you want to send a message to. You can press the up and down arrow to search for the recipient name up and down of the screen.

Siri icon will appear to send your message. Then, dictate your message and Siri will repeat the dictated message back for confirmation.

If what you have said were correct, you can say "Perfect" and order, Siri, to "Send the message". Siri will reply to you that your message has been sent.

How to Setup 3D Map Guide

On CarPlay Homescreen: Tap on Map icon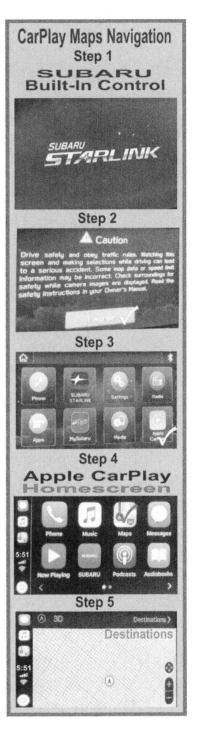

On Map: Tap on **Destinations** at the top right of the screen

On Destination: Select from any of these destinations:

1. **Get directions to a destination in the list:** Choose your Destination by tapping.
2. **Get direction to a nearby service:** Choose Service Category including Coffee, Gas or Parking; and choose the destination.

OR

Use Siri: Ask Siri:

> ➢ Take me to the address in the destination.
> ➢ Take me home
> ➢ Take me to the nearest

155

fueling station or gas station
- ➢ Take me to the nearest hospital
- ➢ Take me to the nearest Shopping Mall
- ➢ Find the nearest hotel
- ➢ Tell me the location of where I am … and many others.

How to Use Map on Your iPhone XR

On Homescreen: Tap on the **Maps** icon.

On Maps: Tap on **Directions**

On Directions: Select

- ✓ **Drive:** If you are driving
- ✓ **Walk:** If you want to trek the distance
- ✓ **Transit:** If you will be taking various transport
- ✓ **Ride:** If you want to embark on the distance with a bicycle, motorcycle, or tricycle.
- ➢ Choose the route you want. Maps will show you the shortest direction with consideration of traffic conditions.
- ➢ Tap on **Go.** For you to see the general overview of your route bearing direction.
- ➢ Tap on **Tap for Overview** in the banner. Also, you may tap on **Share ETA** to share your location with others.
- ➢ To stop the **Navigation,** tap on **End** and tap on **End Route.**

Use Siri: Ask Siri to "**Stop Navigating**" once you have **Hands-Free Activated** (Switched "ON").

How You Can Prevent Tolls or Highways

On Homescreen: Tap on **Settings**

On Settings: Tap on **Maps**

On Maps: Tap on **Driving & Navigation**

On Driving & Navigation: Tap the Activator of **Tolls or Highways**

Hint: As soon as you commence your movement, the Maps will automatically update itself to show you the most appropriate direction.

The hindrance on your route bearing could be seen on Maps iPhone by using your finger to scroll up.

Maps will prevent you from missing your next turn at the beginning and walking out of the route by showing you the perfect lane you should remain when you are driving.

BONUS CHAPTER

The Protective Accessory for iPhone XR

Although, Apple organization has already designed prolong durable iPhone outer ringside to satisfy the user by using a stainless glass body to repel water and easy to clean when it is having contact with hard stain or covered with dust.

But, this is not adequate for those that want the iPhone to be a fully protected incidence that may damage the sensitive screen and the backside of the iPhone.

Apple company only provided partial protection, not total protection that could prevent the iPhone's screen from being damaged when it suddenly falls on a hard pointed surface. As a result, it is very important to provide a more sustainable additional **Screen Protector and quality body Casing**.

Now the choice of providing absolute protection for your iPhone is in your hand. If you are looking for where you could get quality and durable casing or screen protectors, there are many quality and smart iPhone body Case and Screen Protectors on the "Amazon Platform", that will also add beauty to your iPhone look "appearance". Search for anyone you like and make an order.

How to Fix Screen Protector without Bubble on the Screen

Some of the Screen protectors come with a sachet of Wet Wipes and Dry Wipes.

Materials You Need:

Alcohol Swap, or Isopropyl Alcohol, Microfiber Cleaning Cloth (MCC) (e.g., Magicfiber, e-cloth,), Dust Removing Sticker (DRS), Thick Paper Business Card

First Method

1. Switch off your iPhone

2. Use alcohol swap or add small Isopropyl alcohol into clean cotton to clean up the surface of the iPhone screen to remove oil on the screen surface. Ensure you clean from inside to the edges of the iPhone.
3. Use the available MCC to clean the iPhone screen surface from edge to edge to completely remove dust.
4. Use a side of DRS to sweep the screen surface from the top to the bottom of the screen. Just 2 to 3 times (Optional).
5. Remove the protective paper/nylon at the front of the Screen Protector.
6. Gently hold the Screen front the left and right sides with your hand.
7. Slowly bend down the head of the Screen protector toward the head of the iPhone. Use your second hand to support the screen protector at the opposite end to align the screen protector edge with the iPhone top edge.
8. Slowly move your hand by holding the screen down; with the help of the thumb of the second-hand, press the screen surface to remove any possible bubble, and use the Thick Card to slightly press the screen down and sweep the surface toward the bottom of the iPhone side by side as you are moving down your hand to prevent bubble(s).

Second Method

1. Remove the protective nylon or paper on the screen protector surface.
2. Position the side of the screen protector at one side of the iPhone to ensure that the screen is at the center of the iPhone. Some screen protectors come with tape stickers but if you do not have never mind.
3. Position the upper end of the screen protector at the same upper end of your iPhone and gently move down your hand until it gets to the opposite end.
4. Allow it to spread and use the Microfiber Cleaning Cloth to press the screen surface from the top of the iPhone by

moving your hand from left to right till you get to the bottom of the iPhone to prevent a bubble. Or

Third Method: Nylon or Paper Sticker Support Method

> ➤ If you have a paper sticker, cut three of 4cm of paper sticker each. Stick 2cm from the length of the paper sticker at the left, right, and bottom center.
> ➤ Gently position the screen protector top edge at the exact top edge of the iPhone screen.
> ➤ Look at both sides, and ensure the screen protector is aligned with the iPhone edge.
> ➤ Use the remaining 2cm paper sticker at the left and right to adhere to the screen protector with the main iPhone body.
> ➤ Hold the opposite paper sticker to slowly bring down the screen protector to the surface of the iPhone.
> ➤ Use clean soft MCC to rub the surface of the protective screen from left to right to prevent bubbles as shown in the below pictures.

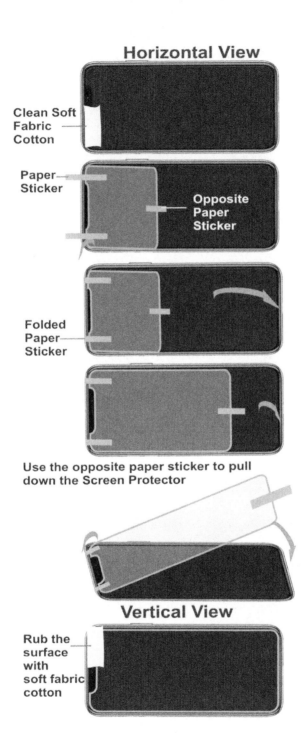

Horizontal View

Clean Soft
Fabric
Cotton

Paper
Sticker

Opposite
Paper
Sticker

Folded
Paper
Sticker

Use the opposite paper sticker to pull
down the Screen Protector

Vertical View

Rub the
surface
with
soft fabric
cotton

161

Gratitude

Thank you for buying this inevitable iPhone Guide companion. I strongly believed that at the end of the reading and application of all the working steps in this manual, you would surely accomplish all your expectations and be happy with using one of the latest iPhone versions.

Printed in Great Britain
by Amazon

74458796R00098